Unchained

Freed to be His Treasure

Kirkland M. Rite

Printed in the United States of America

First Printing: 2025

Eternal Kingdom International Publishing, LLC

LIBRARY OF CONGRESS

LCCN: 2025950716

ISBN- 978-1-968815-09-7 - Paperback

ISBN- 978-1-968815-11-0 - eBook

ISBN- 978-1-968815-12-7 – Audio-book

ISBN - 978-1-968815-10-3 – Hardback - Case laminate

ISBN - 978-1-968815-17-2 – Cloth-bound Hardcover with Dust jacket

Other Works by Kirkland M. Rite:

- *Unchained: Freed to be His Treasure* EKI Publishing 2025
- *Baptized: Why Did I Get Wet* EKI Publishing Coming 2026

Where the Spirit of the Lord is, there is freedom. And we all, with unveiled faces, behold His glory, being transformed into the same image from glory to glory - by the Spirit of the Lord.

-   2 Corinthians 3 : 17 - 18

Dedication:

To my beloved wife -Your unwavering strength, quiet intercession, and fearless love have been the steady fire behind every word I write. You have stood not only beside me, but before me in battle, covering me when I had no words, no answers, no strength left to give.

To my children - You are not simply the legacy I leave behind; you are the arrows I send forward. Your faith, your sacrifice, and your joy have made this journey holy. You have ministered not just as sons and daughters, but as carriers of the same mantle - overcomers in your own right.

This book was never written by one man.

It is the sound of a family in covenant with heaven.

A house determined to live the message we preach.

Together, we not only survived but also thrived.

We overcame.

Kirkland M. Rite

Foreword

By *Adam S. Bradford,*

In maintaining a good relationship, especially that of marriage, one must remind their significant other of how important they are, and in return, be reminded of their worth as well. In the essence of time, we can become despondent to that critical need with the daily grind of life's itineraries, thus taking for granted the presence and purpose of those around us, and even the purpose of ourselves. In becoming carried away with the worries of this world, we tend to lose focus of our freedom that was bestowed upon us at the cross and our identity that followed in the Resurrection. We begin to forget our well-washed worth as we return only to wallow about in the filthy mire, in which its chains of shame lie in wait much like that of the high priest Joshua in the book of Zechariah, hoping to adorn us as well with dung-covered rags along with the accusations of Satan.

But as Joshua felt the love of God cleanse and re-clothe him in the presence of the heavenly hosts, reminding Israel of His love and commitment, we are also reminded in the book of Lamentations that the mercies of the Lord are renewed every morning. Kirkland's book is a love letter from God, reminding the reader that they are loved well beyond the lies that this broken world has entangled them with. Kirkland gives many insightful examples into his life's ministry that I could relate to, and especially that of his childhood experience with his parents that had weighed heavily on him into his adult life.

May this book be a blessing of freedom and that of unwavering peace that surpasses all understanding to all who read it.

Adam Bradford,

Author of

The United States of Apostasy

We Have Seen Them

Encounters of Destiny

The Angel's Winepress

When the Last Cowboy is Gone

The Law of The Lamb.

Contents

A

Introduction

The Sound of Broken Chains

The chains are already broken. Jesus shattered them at the cross. But people will try to heap those fragments back onto you, until you begin to wear broken chains as if they still bind you. This book will teach you to drop what has already been destroyed, to refuse the prison of shame, and to walk unchained in your true design.

Chains are not always forged from iron. Some are forged from whispers, from labels, from memories that refuse to die. They are the invisible shackles that cling to your name, wrapping themselves around your future until you believe you will never be free.

But this is why Jesus came. At the cross, He broke the chains no man could carry, crushing the written verdict that stood against us and nailing it to the wood. In that moment, He stripped the powers and made a public spectacle of them (Colossians 2:14-15). If you have not yet found that freedom, know this: it is not far from you. It is found in a born-again encounter with Jesus, the new birth that opens the eyes to see the Kingdom (John 3:3). In Him, the old self is buried, and what rises is not patched together but brand new - a restored image, a resurrected design (2 Corinthians 5:17).

I know a man who lived beneath such chains. His story is not neat or polished. At eighteen, one decision - immature, regrettable, and life-altering - branded him with a scarlet letter. He confessed. He repented. He faced his sentence. But when his time was done, the sentence did not end. Everywhere he went, the whispers followed. The registry marked his name, but worse than that, religion marked his soul. Pastors told him, *"Your ministry is over."* Congregations looked at him not with mercy, but with suspicion. Even when he lifted his hands in worship, he felt their eyes weighing him down.

He was born again - remade by God - yet treated as if the old man still lived. Free in Christ but chained in the courts of human opinion.

Perhaps you know that weight. Perhaps you, too, have been reduced to the worst thing you ever did, or the cruelest rumor ever spread about you. Perhaps your name has been dragged through the mud until it feels nailed to your skin. Perhaps you know the sting of sitting in the back row, praying no one notices you, afraid the spotlight might reveal your scars.

Religion whispers, *"You are finished."* Shame hisses, *"You will never change."* But the Spirit of God declares, *"Your design is eternal, and My call is irrevocable."*

You can almost hear it.

The faint rattle of metal against stone. The dragging echo of links that were never meant to be carried this long.

Some chains are forged by others - words spoken in anger, labels handed down by family, judgments carved into your name by religion or culture. Some chains we forge ourselves - through sin, through compromise, through shame that won't release its grip.

And though Jesus shattered those chains at the cross, many of us still live as though they are intact. We drag what has already been destroyed. We allow people to heap them back upon our shoulders. We decorate them. We normalize them. We make prisons of our past and call them home.

But the voice of heaven still whispers, urgent and tender: *"You were not born for bondage. You were born again for freedom."*

Beyond Forgiveness

The message of this book is not merely that you can be forgiven - though forgiveness is wondrous. The heartbeat of *Unchained* is that you can be reborn. You can be resurrected into the image you were always meant to carry.

As David Webb describes, the new birth is not the invention of a new man but the resurrection of the original design - the restoration of humanity's first nature before sin distorted it.

(Webb, 2025b) [1] The "new creation" Paul speaks of is really the original blueprint God dreamed before the foundation of the world. To be born again is to be awakened - not into something foreign, but into something familiar. It is God breathing again into dust, reviving what was buried, restoring what was broken.

When you are born again, you are not patched up. You are not merely pardoned. You are restored. Reconstructed. Resurrected. You are not a broken version limping forward - you are a son, a daughter, reborn into the family you were always destined to belong to.

This is not about polishing your image. It is not about pretending your chains are harmless. It is not even about forgiveness alone.

But let this be clear: the gospel does not declare, *"You are perfect as you are."* That is the lie of a culture that wants affirmation without transformation. The cross is not God's stamp of approval on the old man; it is His verdict of death upon it. The old nature must be crucified with its lusts and affections (Galatians 5:24). What rises is not the self that sinned, but the self reborn - the new creation, the resurrected image, the garden nature restored.

Do not polish your chains and call them jewelry. Do not hang your shackles around your neck and call them personality.

---

[1]David S. Webb, *Escape the Shame of Babylon* (EKI Publishing, 2025)

4

The cross is not for decoration; it is for execution. And what it kills, Christ raises brand new.

Romans 8:15 says it plainly: *"The Spirit you received does not make you slaves, so that you live in fear again; rather, the Spirit you received brought about your adoption to sonship."* The Spirit does not hand you a probation card. He hands you a birth certificate. He does not give you permission to live small; He gives you power to live as an heir.

The Man I Know

I think again of the man I know. When the world said, *"Sit down and do nothing,"* he obeyed a greater voice that said, *"Rise and build."* He and his wife opened the doors of a small church in a borrowed building. He did not want a stage; he wanted a place for the broken to gather. People came. Lives changed. Over the years, thousands repented, were baptized, and experienced the Spirit of God in ways they had never known.

And yet - even in the midst of revival, the whispers chased him. His past became a weapon in the mouths of religious people. Threats came against his life. He was told again and again, *"Your name disqualifies you."*

But God whispered something else. One night, in the silence of his despair, he heard the Spirit say, *"You are My treasure in a field. You are My pearl of great price. I sold everything to purchase you"* (Matthew 13:44-46).

That man learned that freedom does not come from erasing your past but from refusing to let your past define your name. His story is proof that the Kingdom does not choose the qualified - it resurrects the broken.

The Chains We Carry

You may not carry his story, but you carry your own. Different details, same chains.

For some, it is the memory of failure. For others, the betrayal of someone you trusted. For still others, it is the gnawing shame of addiction, divorce, abuse, or rejection. We learn to wear masks and call them personalities. We learn to bury wounds and call them maturity. But inside, the chains rattle every time we try to move forward.

This book is written for you. For the one who wonders if they will always be defined by what was done to them. For the one who fears they will always be remembered for what they did. For the one who feels more like an exile than a child of God.

Unchained is not for the polished. It is for the marked. For the misfits. For the remnant who will not settle for religion that entertains their wounds but never heals them.

The Promise

From the very beginning, God breathed His image into humanity (Genesis 1:26-27). He called us sons and daughters. Sin tried to distort that image, but the cross was never about giving you a role to play - it was about giving you back your name. Jesus did not come to make bad people behave better. He came to resurrect dead people into life. To awaken the overcomer inside you that has been buried under shame.

And so the Spirit still whispers: *"You are not what you did. You are not what they said. You are not the label. You are My design, reborn. My child, resurrected. My treasure, restored."*

This book is not a manual of self-help or hollow affirmations. It is a call to resurrection. It will not teach you how to decorate your chains; it will show you how to leave them in the grave. It will not whisper, "You are fine as you are"; it will thunder, "You are a new creation in Christ."

This book will teach you to drop what has already been destroyed, to refuse the prison of shame, and to walk unchained in your true design. It will train you to hear the difference between the old man's voice and the Spirit's. It will call forth your new nature, not affirm your fallen one.

This book will walk with you into the places where shame hides. It will confront the lies that have been whispered over your life. It will call you back to the higher ground of your true design. And it will echo the decree of Heaven over your soul:

Unchained.

Invocation

Breathe, child of God - lay the weight down. The chains you brought here cannot follow you out. You are more than whispers and labels; you are Heaven's design, reborn in fire, resurrected in love.

So I speak this over you now in the name of Jesus:

Rise.

Remember.

Return to your original name.

Let every false verdict be silenced. Let every chain of shame shatter. Let the King's whisper be the only voice that holds you: "You are Mine. You are free. You are unchained."

Lord, break every chain of false affirmation that would tether us to the flesh. Silence echoes of past chains. Teach us to die with You and to rise with You, to walk in the Spirit and not the flesh. Destroy the lies of our old man's sentence and declare the new creation's truth. Let this book be an altar where shackles fall and a training ground where sons and daughters stand.

Amen.

Scripture Index

Chapter One

Who Am I Really?

Sit with this for a moment: The most important question of your life isn't, *"What am I supposed to do?"* or *"Where should I go?"* The question echoing beneath every heartbeat is simpler - but far more powerful:

Who am I?

We spend so much of our lives chasing titles and roles. We collect them like trophies on a dusty shelf: son, daughter, employee, leader, failure, overachiever, outsider, star.

Sometimes, we don't even realize we're wearing them. We slip them on so naturally, like an old coat. We accept them from voices that never truly knew us - teachers, parents, ex-lovers, bosses, critics, or that harsh inner narrator whispering late at night. We start believing these labels define us.

But when the noise fades, when you're alone and staring at the ceiling in the dark, there it is - that whisper:

Who am I really?

The Weight of a Name

I still remember a Christmas when I was five years old. It's woven into me like a hidden thread in a favorite shirt.

That year, I had a rare chance to go to the store alone with my mom. For a little boy, that felt like a private adventure, like stepping into a grown-up world where you're trusted and seen.

We were picking out a Christmas gift for my brother. My mom chose a record player, and though I didn't fully grasp its magic yet, I knew it was important.

At the checkout, she knelt down, locked her eyes onto mine - sharp, soft, and sacred all at once - and said, *"Don't tell your brother what it is."*

I nodded so hard it felt like my head might pop off. In that moment, I felt like a soldier entrusted with a nation's secrets. My chest swelled with pride.

But secrets are heavy, especially when you're small. They rattle around in your chest, hum in your mind, and burn on your tongue.

As Christmas got closer, my brother started his gentle, crafty questioning: *"What is it? Tell me just one thing! Just a tiny hint!"*

At first, I stood strong. I wore my secret like armor. But then, in a tiny crack of weakness, I let it slip.

"It plays records," I blurted out.

His eyes went wide, his whole face lighting up like a fireworks show. *"It's a record player!"* he yelled, then bolted out of the room, practically flying with excitement.

I stood frozen, my heart crashing like waves in a storm. The secret I'd sworn to guard had slipped right through my small hands.

My dad didn't yell. He didn't slam doors or deliver harsh lectures. He looked at me with steady, quiet eyes that saw all the way through me.

Then he spoke words that etched themselves into my spirit:

"That's not what Rites do."

It wasn't about a gift. It wasn't even about obedience. It was about identity - about what it meant to carry the Rite name.

In that moment, I understood that being a son wasn't just about sharing a last name or sitting at the same dinner table. It was about carrying a legacy. It was about trust. It was about living in a way that honored the family name, a name bigger than just me.

Names We Carry

Many of us walk through life carrying names and labels we didn't choose: *Rejected. Unworthy. Not enough. Too broken.*

We pick up these names from moments of failure, from words spoken in anger, from relationships that fell apart, from the dark corners of our own minds. Some names hold a weight that shapes the course of our lives.

But there is a better name waiting for you - a name whispered over your soul since before you took your first breath.

When you are born again, you receive a new identity. You aren't just handed a spiritual insurance policy or a ticket out of trouble. You are given a new name, a new spirit, a new breath.

Scripture says you were made in God's image (Genesis 1:27). Let that sink in. The same God who carved oceans and designed sunsets, who calls stars by name and holds galaxies together - He made you to reflect Him.

When you are born again, His breath ignites something inside you that was asleep for too long. You don't become a slightly improved version of your old self; you become a brand-new creation (2 Corinthians 5:17).

As Kevin Rice explains in *Cultivating the New Nature*: *"In Greek, the word for 'regeneration' is paliggenesia… meaning 'again' + 'birth, beginning.' Through the new birth, God has re-Genesis-ed mankind, restoring the spiritual man back to the original garden nature He intended at creation."* (Rice, 2023a) [2]

The old man - the flesh with its sins, verdicts, and false names - is not affirmed. It is crucified. Buried. What God raises is not the self that sinned, but the self reborn: Spirit-born, resurrected, alive.

---

[2] Kevin Rice, *Cultivating the New Nature* (EKI Publishing, 2023)

This is not about polishing your image or hiding flaws better. It is about resurrection. The spark of the divine nature of God, breathed into you from creation, comes alive. Your old self dies - the self that carried all those false names and heavy labels - and a new, radiant, Spirit-born you rises.

The Whisper of Belonging

I remember one night when I was alone, after a particularly hard day. I felt empty. All the old voices came roaring back: *"You're failing. You're not enough. You'll never get it right."*

But in that stillness, I felt a deeper whisper. It was gentle but unyielding, like a steady hand on my shoulder:

"You're Mine. You're My child. You carry My breath. You are loved beyond measure."

I broke. Not in a way that destroyed me, but in a way that set me free.

The new name God gives you isn't earned by behavior or religious performance. It's a gift, freely given because He loves you.

David Webb once wrote: *"You are a chosen generation, a royal priesthood, a holy nation, God's own possession... Heaven has already recorded your name."* (Webb, 2025c) [3]

You don't need to claw your way into God's favor. You simply step into who you already are.

---

[3] David Webb, *The Unique Factor* (EKI Publishing, 2025)

15

Living From Belovedness

Henri Nouwen wrote, *"Your true identity is as a child of God. This is the identity you have to accept. Once you claim it and settle in it, you can live your life as one who is deeply loved."* (Nouwen, 1992) [4]

Brennan Manning echoed: *"Define yourself radically as one beloved by God. This is the true self. Every other identity is illusion."* (Manning, 1994)[5]

And as Kevin Rice expands in *Cultivating the New Nature*: *"Each newborn child of God has such great potential that a single chapter couldn't begin to explain what a newborn is capable of becoming."* (Rice, 2023a) [6]

You don't live for approval. You live from belovedness. You don't strive for identity. You walk in it.

And when you say, *"I am,"* you are not echoing the fallen man that must be crucified. You are echoing the resurrected voice of your new nature. God does not affirm the old self; He buries it. What He raises is holy, Spirit-born, and free.

The Father's Voice

The first sound you ever knew was not the cry of your birth - it was the voice that called you *mine*. Before your name was spoken on earth, it was written in Heaven. You were never

---

[4] Henri J.M. Nouwen, *Life of the Beloved* (Crossroad Publishing, 1992)
[5] Brennan Manning, *Abba's Child: The Cry of the Heart for Intimate Belonging* (NavPress, 1994).
[6] Kevin Rice, *Cultivating the New Nature* (EKI Publishing, 2023)

abandoned to wander through this world trying to earn belonging. You were born into a Father's gaze that never looked away.

The world will try to rename you. Failure. Forgotten. Forsaken. But the Father still whispers over every wound: *"You are My child."* Not a project. Not a problem. A son. A daughter. A living reflection of His own breath.

You are not the orphan trying to find a home; you are the home He chooses to dwell in. The Spirit within you cries, *"Abba, Father,"* and Heaven answers back, *"Yes, you are Mine."* (Romans 8:15-16)

So lift your head. You were never meant to scrape for identity - you were meant to walk in inheritance. Let the chains of confusion fall. Let the noise of unworthiness fade. Hear it again, the same words that framed creation and still echo through redemption:

"I will not leave you comfortless; I will come to you." (John 14:18)

You are His. Always have been. Always will be.

Scripture Index

#IAmHis

#SpiritBorn

#Unchained

Apostolic Equipping:
How to Speak Identity Over Others

When someone speaks from the old nature - words of shame, regret, or self-condemnation - do not agree with it. The cross has buried that voice. Instead, answer with the truth of the Spirit-born life:

- To a spouse weighed down by failure: *"That old verdict is dead. You are alive in Christ, chosen and beloved."*
- To a child wrestling with fear: *"Fear belongs to the old self. You are Spirit-filled, brave, and never alone."*
- To a friend drowning in regret: *"Your past was crucified with Christ. What lives now is forgiven, new, and free."*

We do not echo the voice of the flesh; we declare the resurrection life of the Spirit. This is how chains break - not by affirming what died, but by calling forth what God has raised.

Chapter Two

What Was I Made For?

The world is quick to tell you what you are good for.

A job title.

A grade on a paper.

A role in the family.

A place in the system.

But deeper than all of that is the ache every soul carries:

What was I made for?

A Walk Into the Question

I still remember an evening walk, the sun slipping low, the air painted in oranges and purples. My heart was heavy, but the quiet made room for God's whisper:

"What if your greatest impact isn't what you do for people, but who you become with Me?"

It stopped me in my tracks. For so long, I had measured purpose in achievements and output. But that whisper cut through the noise - what if purpose is not about what you produce but about who you are becoming?

The Ache of Insignificance

David knew this ache. To his father, he was the youngest boy - a shepherd left with "those few sheep" (1 Samuel 17:28). To his brothers, he was insignificant, more nuisance than warrior. To his community, he was just another son of Jesse.

But in the fields, away from the noise, David discovered a whisper. Alone with his harp and his sheep, he began to hear what heaven had written about him long before anyone else could see it.

The world called him insignificant.

God called him king.

The Lie of Worthlessness

Maybe you've felt it too - the sense that what you do doesn't matter, that your life is a string of accidents, that your existence is nothing more than survival.

I know a man who carried that same weight. As a boy, he heard again and again that he was an "accident waiting to happen." Every failure seemed to confirm it. Every wrong turn echoed it louder. And over time, he began to wear that phrase like a skin.

But lies, no matter how loud, do not get the final word.

When he remembered who his Father was - when he remembered that design had come before sin, that intention had come before failure - something broke open in him. He realized what you must realize, too: you are not an accident. You are purpose wrapped in flesh. You are design waiting to unfold.

As A.W. Tozer once said, *"The deepest question is not 'What is the will of God for my life?' but rather, 'Who is God, and how can I align my life with Him?'"*(Tozer, 1948) [7]

When you know Him, you begin to know what you were made for.

Ordinary Purposes, Eternal Weight

We often imagine purpose as a singular, world-shaking mission. But sometimes purpose is beautifully ordinary:

- Raising a family that knows God's kindness.
- Encouraging a co-worker who feels unseen.
- Creating art that reflects Heaven's beauty.
- Allowing God to heal you in a hidden season.

Your purpose is not a puzzle to solve. It is a relationship to grow into.

Jesus Himself lived thirty years before He ever preached a sermon or worked a miracle. Thirty hidden years, marked not by noise but by faithfulness. And yet every day of those thirty years was purpose - a son growing in wisdom and stature, in favor with God and man (Luke 2:52).

If even the Son of God could live decades in obscurity before His public assignment, your hidden years are not wasted. They are pregnant with purpose.

---

[7] A.W. Tozer, *The Pursuit of God* (Camp Hill, PA: Christian Publications, 1948).

Resurrected Design

Being born again does not simply give you a new task - it awakens your original design. You were not made to merely fill space. You were made to reflect the glory of the One who breathed into you (Genesis 1:27; Genesis 2:7).

Paul declares it this way: *"We are His workmanship, created in Christ Jesus for good works, which God prepared beforehand that we should walk in them"* (Ephesians 2:10). You are not stumbling through life, hoping to matter. You are God's craftsmanship, carved by intention, resurrected for purpose.

Kevin Rice explains in *Cultivating the New Nature*: *"The newborn nature is limitless in its potential when it's placed in a proper environment to grow. All things are given in seed form and must be cultivated."* (Rice, 2023a) [8]

As C.S. Lewis wrote, *"The Son of God became man to enable men to become sons of God."* [(Lewis, 1952)] [9] And sons do not wander aimlessly. Sons walk in inheritance. Daughters walk in design.

More Than a Role

The enemy will always try to chain you to function instead of identity. *"You are what you do. You are what you fail to do. You are your past. You are your mistakes."*

But the Kingdom flips this upside down:

---

[8] Kevin Rice, *Cultivating the New Nature* (EKI Publishing, 2023).
[9] C.S. Lewis, *Mere Christianity* (United Kingdom: Geoffrey Bles, 1952)

- You do not work for identity - you work from identity.

- You do not fight for favor - you fight from favor.

- You do not search for meaning - you live from meaning already given.

David didn't fight Goliath to prove himself. He fought because heaven had already whispered who he was. The stone in his sling was not aimed by skill alone; it was carried by design.

David Webb reflects this truth in *The Unique Factor*: *"Before I formed you in the womb, I knew you… Every page exists because You first wrote the eternal script of our lives."* (Webb, 2025c) [10]

A Moment of Belovedness

I remember one day, standing under the spray of a shower after what felt like the unraveling of everything. Finances collapsing. Ministry attacked. Threats in the air. Roadblocks everywhere I turned. The water ran down my face like a flood I couldn't escape.

And in that moment - when I had no song, no strength, no sermon - I heard Him.

"You are My favorite."

The words undid me. I broke and wept as the water washed over me, feeling the weight roll from my chest. But before I could even breathe out my thanks, He spoke again:

"You are not My only favorite. They all are."

---

[10] David Webb, *The Unique Factor* (EKI Publishing, 2025)

It struck me like lightning and comfort all at once. His heart is wide enough for every child. His design does not play favorites, but somehow, in His love, each of us is His favorite.

That day, I realized I wasn't made for performance or perfection. I was made for belovedness. And so are you.

And when you declare *"I am"* in these moments, remember: you are not echoing the old self that must be crucified. You are echoing the resurrected voice of the Spirit-born nature. The flesh was condemned; the Spirit is adopted, filled with God's breath, and free.

What Was I Made For

When the noise quiets and the world stops demanding, the Father still asks a question - soft, steady, almost hidden beneath your breath: *"Do you know what I made you for today?"*

Purpose doesn't always roar. Sometimes it whispers.
It may look like choosing gentleness when anger feels easier, or forgiveness when bitterness feels justified. It may be a word of kindness that seems small but shifts the atmosphere of a room. It may even be rest - the kind that says, "I trust You enough to stop."

Purpose rarely arrives in a spotlight; it often walks in through obedience. You were not made to chase destiny as if it's somewhere far away. You were made to carry it, here and now, in every ordinary act made sacred by love.

You don't wait for purpose - you walk in it. One step. One choice. One moment at a time. That is holy ground. That is why you're here.

Scripture Index

#OriginalDesign

#SpiritBorn

#Unchained

Apostolic Equipping:

Practices to Recover Purpose

Purpose is not discovered by staring at yourself in a mirror. It is revealed as the Spirit bears witness in you and through others. Here are practices to help recover and walk in your purpose:

- **Pause and Ask** - Take time with God daily and pray: *"Father, what did You make me for today?"*

- **Invite Others to Speak** - Ask two trusted believers: *"What grace do you see on my life? Where do you see God's hand on me?"* Apostolic culture builds in teams, not isolation.

- **Discern and Act** - Don't just collect insights. Act on them. Purpose matures as you walk in it - one faithful step at a time.

- **Break the Old Voice** - When purposeless thoughts arise, silence them: *"That was crucified with Christ. I am God's workmanship, raised for good works."*

We do not affirm purposelessness; we cultivate Spirit-born design together.

Chapter Three

When Am I?

We are obsessed with time.

When will I get there? When will I be free? When will I finally overcome?

We imagine overcoming as a finish line shimmering on the horizon, always out ahead of us, waiting for the day when we're strong enough, holy enough, disciplined enough.

But the Spirit speaks differently.

John wrote it not as a command but as a fact:

"You are of God, little children, and have overcome them, because greater is He that is in you than he that is in the world" (1 John 4:4).

Notice the tense. Not *you will*. Not *you might*. Not *you should*. But *you have*.

In God's eyes, victory is not a distant someday. It is a present reality. It is not a reward for endurance - it is the birthmark of being born again.

The Wilderness of Delay

The Israelites knew what it was to wrestle with time. Freed from Egypt's whip, they stood at the edge of promise. The land flowed with milk and honey. Grapes so large they needed two men to carry them hung from the vine. The fragrance of inheritance drifted in the air.

And yet, fear drowned out faith. Ten spies filled the camp with despair: *"The people are stronger than we are… the land devours its inhabitants"* (Numbers 13:31-32).

But two voices cut through the noise. Joshua and Caleb tore their clothes and declared: *"If the Lord delights in us, He will bring us into this land… do not fear them. Their protection has departed from them, and the Lord is with us"* (Numbers 14:8-9).

Caleb already saw himself across the river. He carried tomorrow's victory in today's breath. He lived not in delay but in destiny.

But the people chose fear. And the result was devastating: forty years circling sand, forty years of funerals, forty years of delay. A whole generation died in the wilderness not because they lacked strength, but because they refused perspective.

That is the cost of unbelief. Destiny delayed does not simply stall your life - it can bury it. How many promises have gone unclaimed, how many inheritances left untouched, not because God was unwilling, but because His people refused to believe?

The Chains of Delay

Delay is not only about calendars. It is about chains.

Freedom can feel postponed when the echoes of old bondage still rattle in our ears. Israel was already free from Pharaoh's whip, yet in their hearts they were still slaves. They stood on the edge of promise but saw themselves through the eyes of captivity. The chains had been broken, but they still dragged them in their minds.

That is the tension of timing: Christ breaks the chain in a moment, but learning to live without dragging it behind you is a process. Being born again is instantaneous; walking unchained is a journey marked by stages. Heaven declares "free" long before your heart learns how to feel free.

The Grasshopper Vision

Among the spies' words was one phrase that dripped poison into Israel's bones: *"We seemed like grasshoppers in our own eyes, and we looked the same to them"* (Numbers 13:33).

This was not just fear. It was identity collapse. They no longer saw themselves as sons of Abraham, heirs of promise, children of covenant. They saw themselves as insects. Small. Weak. Disposable.

The enemy didn't even need to swing a sword. Israel defeated itself with its own self-perception.

And this tragedy did not end there. Generations later, when Israel again faced invading armies, the language returned. Judges records that the Midianites and Amalekites swarmed *"like locusts"* - like grasshoppers - covering the land (Judges 6:5; Judges 7:12).

What their fathers saw in themselves, their children now saw in their enemies. Their vision had shrunk even further than it was when they first entered the land. Grasshopper vision had become generational.

Here is the tragedy: when you do not break free of distorted identity, you pass down fear instead of faith. What you call yourself in one generation becomes what your children face in the next.

Caleb's Faith Across a Lifetime

And yet Caleb's faith did not die in the wilderness. Decades later, when Israel finally crossed the Jordan and claimed much of the land, Caleb came forward at age eighty-five and declared:

"I am still as strong today as the day Moses sent me out; I am just as vigorous to go out to battle now as I was then. Now give me this hill country that the Lord promised me… the Lord helping me, I will drive them out just as He said" (Joshua 14:10-12).

Eighty-five years old. A lifetime of waiting. Surrounded by funerals, carrying memory after memory of delay. And yet his confession had not changed. He still saw himself not as a grasshopper but as an heir.

Caleb understood what most of Israel missed: time does not erode promise. What God speaks is eternal. The calendar does not weaken His word. You can bury the body of a generation, but you cannot bury the word of the Lord.

Already, Not Yet

This is why God speaks victory in past tense. *"You have overcome."* Because the greatest battle is not against giants or Midianites or armies without number. The greatest battle is over perspective.

At the cross, Jesus cried, *"It is finished"* (John 19:30). Not someday. Not eventually. Finished. The written verdict against you was nailed to the wood and disarmed forever (Colossians 2:14-15).

Andrew Murray once said, *"God is ready to assume full responsibility for the life wholly yielded to Him."* (Murray, 1982) [11] Victory is not achieved by our striving; it is received by our surrender. To yield is to realize: I am not echoing the condemned flesh - I am echoing the Spirit-born life God has already declared over me.

Corrie Ten Boom put it simply: *"Never be afraid to trust an unknown future to a known God."* (Ten Boom, 1982) [12] Your future is not a mystery to Him. It is already secured in His word.

---

[11] Andrew Murray, *Absolute Surrender* (New Kensington, PA: Whitaker House, 1982).
[12] Corrie Ten Boom, *Clippings from My Notebook* (Old Tappan, NJ: Fleming H. Revell, 1982).

Metamorphosis: From Glory to Glory

And yet, while victory is present, **formation is progressive**. The seed is true from the moment it's sown, but oak takes time.

Kevin Rice captures this rhythm of grace:

"As we place this new nature in an environment saturated with the Presence of God, we begin to be transformed… It's not instantaneous; it's gradual. We change and progress from one degree of glory to another." (Rice, 2023a) [13]

This is the tension we live in: the **now** of identity and the **becoming** of maturity; the verdict is settled, the vessel is still being shaped. The Spirit witnesses *who you are* while also shepherding *who you are becoming*. Both are holy.

So don't despise slow. The Kingdom often moves at the speed of roots. Hidden seasons are not empty; they are incubators. Keep your new nature in the **Presence environment** - worship, the Word, communion with the saints - and you will watch today's "already" unfold into tomorrow's "also."

A Man Out of Time

I know a man who spent years believing his time had passed. Mistakes chained him. Accusations shadowed him. Every opportunity felt blocked, as if heaven had placed him on probation.

---

[13] Kevin Rice, *Cultivating the New Nature* (EKI Publishing, 2023)

But one night, in prayer, he sensed the Lord whisper: *"You are not waiting on your time. Your time is waiting on you."*

That revelation split him open. He realized the same Spirit that raised Jesus from the dead already lived inside him (Romans 8:11). The future he thought he had forfeited was still alive in God's now. He wasn't waiting on victory. Victory was waiting on him to walk in it.

Now Is the Time

There comes a moment when the waiting ends. When heaven stops speaking in future tense and starts whispering, *"Now."*

You were not reborn for delay. You were born again into a present victory. The same Spirit that raised Jesus from the dead doesn't visit you someday - it inhabits you now. You are not a grasshopper among giants; you are an heir among promises. The same ground that once looked impossible will one day bear your footprints.

You live under *"It is finished,"* not *"maybe someday."* Transformation is not an event waiting on your perfection - it's a Presence already shaping your reflection. You are being changed from glory to glory, not by effort, but by exposure. Every time you linger near His Presence, your new nature breathes a little deeper, grows a little stronger, shines a little steadier.

So stop circling what He has already given. Stop waiting for permission when Heaven already said, *"Go."* You are not waiting for freedom. You are not waiting for purpose. You are not waiting for your time.

You are free. You are His. You are unchained.

So root deep. Grow slow. Shine steady. Let tomorrow's victory echo in today's lungs. This is the hour. This is the moment. Not someday. Not almost. Now.

Scripture Index

#NowIsTheTime

#SpiritBorn

#Unchained

.

Apostolic Equipping:
How to Walk With Someone in Delay

Waiting seasons can feel like prisons, but they can also become sanctuaries. When walking with a friend in delay, resist the urge to hand them clichés. Instead, help them anchor in God's proven record:

- **Listen before speaking.** Sit with them in silence if needed. Presence matters more than answers.

- **Point to God's history.** Remind them of chains already broken in their past - proof that He has not stopped working.

- **Pray resurrection truth.** Don't tell them simply to "be patient." Speak over them: *"The old verdict is dead. You are Spirit-born, and His promise is alive."*

- **Stay consistent.** Delay feels endless; your steady encouragement can become their reminder that God's timeline has not failed.

This is how we walk each other through wilderness seasons - not by affirming delay as destiny, but by declaring that God is faithful and His promise is still alive.

Chapter Four

I Am

Two of the most dangerous words you will ever speak are these:

"I am…"

Whatever follows those words begins to shape the way you see yourself, the way you move through the world, the way you expect God to treat you.

I am a failure.

I am unloved.

I am broken.

I am forgotten.

I am beyond repair.

These are more than phrases. They are prisons. Each "I am" becomes a chain, a verdict, a false prophecy we live under.

But here is the good news: every false "I am" can be broken, because there is One who declared before time itself, *"I AM WHO I AM"* (Exodus 3:14).

Identity Clarification:

When you say *"I am,"* you are not echoing the fallen man that must be crucified. You are echoing the resurrected voice of your new nature. God does not affirm the old self; He buries it. What He raises is holy, Spirit-born, and free.

But there is something even weightier at stake. God names Himself *"I AM WHO I AM"* (Exodus 3:14). That means every time we declare *"I am…"* we are, in a sense, tying our identity to His Name.

Being made in His image - and being born again to reflect that image and glory - means we must be careful: whatever we attach to *"I am"* is something we are attributing to His reflection in us.

This connects directly to the Third Commandment: *"You shall not take the name of the Lord your God in vain"* (Exodus 20:7). In Hebrew, "name" (*shem*) does not only mean a label; it means authority, reputation, or essence. And "vain" (*shav*) does not primarily mean cursing - it means emptiness, falsehood, or attributing what is empty and untrue to God.

So when we speak over ourselves a false *"I am"* - *"I am worthless," "I am unlovable," "I am beyond repair"* - we are not only lying about ourselves; we are misrepresenting the God whose image we bear. It is as if we are saying God Himself is those things.

But when we declare *"I am Spirit-born," "I am beloved," "I am chosen,"* we are rightly bearing His Name - attaching truth to His authority, reflecting His reality in us.

To misuse *"I am"* is to take the Lord's Name in vain. To declare *"I am"* in alignment with Heaven is to hallow His Name.

But let me add another layer. Some people don't only confuse their old sins with their identity - they also confuse their titles. They say, *"I am the pastor. I am the manager. I am the worship leader."* Those are not who you are; those are only assignments for a season.

Do not confuse the mantle God gives you for a season with the name He has spoken over you forever.

I once went through this myself. The job I had trained for and loved was suddenly gone. One morning I walked into the office and fired myself. The next day I woke up and realized I had nowhere to go. I had wrapped so much of my identity in my position that when it was stripped away, I no longer knew who I was. What followed was a long season of rediscovering that positions are temporary, but identity in Christ is eternal.

This is why Paul's words in 1 Corinthians 13:12 strike so deeply: *"Then I shall know fully, even as I am fully known."* For years, I wrestled with what that meant, until one day the Lord whispered: "You shall be known as you are known by Me."

In the end, it will not be your title, your accolades, or the things this world stamps on you that define you. You will be known by the relationship you carry with Him. That is the identity that endures. That is the name no chain can ever erase.

The God Who Is

When Moses trembled before the burning bush, afraid to go, afraid to speak, he asked the question every human heart eventually asks: *"Who are You?"*

And God answered: *"I AM WHO I AM."*

Not *I was.*

Not *I will be.*

But **I AM.**

The ground of all being. The eternal Presence. The One whose existence is not borrowed but blazing.

A.W. Tozer once wrote: *"God does not derive His being from any source outside Himself. He is self-existent."* (Tozer, 1961) 14

This matters because every "I am" we speak must either align with Him or war against Him. The truth is this: only when your "I am" is rooted in His "I AM" does it carry life.

When "I Am" Becomes a Lie

Israel proved how dangerous misaligned "I ams" can be. Standing at the edge of promise, they said: *"We are like grasshoppers in our own sight"* (Numbers 13:33).

Their "I am" crippled them more than any enemy could. They spoke smallness over themselves until smallness became their truth.

---

14 A.W. Tozer, *The Knowledge of the Holy* (New York: HarperCollins, 1961)

Generations later, the prophet Isaiah confessed: *"Woe to me! I am ruined… I am a man of unclean lips"* (Isaiah 6:5). His "I am" exposed his sin but also his despair. Yet God did not leave him there. A coal from the altar touched his lips, and his "I am ruined" became "Here am I, send me" (Isaiah 6:8).

Every false "I am" can be undone by the touch of the true I AM.

The Labels We Wear

I know a woman who lived for years under the label: *"I am not enough."* Every relationship confirmed it. Every failure screamed it louder. She carried it into church pews and prayer meetings, whispering it even when no one else could hear.

But one night in worship, as she wept under the weight of that phrase, the Spirit whispered a different one: *"You are Mine."*

The chain snapped. The old "I am" was silenced. And from that day forward, she began to rewrite her vocabulary:

- I am beloved (Ephesians 1:6).
- I am chosen (John 15:16).
- I am free (John 8:36).
- I am His (Isaiah 43:1).

This is the pattern of heaven: lies broken, truth declared, chains shattered by the sound of belonging.

Born Again Into a New "I Am"

When you are born again, your "I am" is no longer chained to your past. It is resurrected into Christ's "I AM."

Paul understood this. Once he declared, *"I am the least of the apostles"* (1 Corinthians 15:9). Yet after encountering Christ, he also declared, *"I am what I am by the grace of God"* (1 Corinthians 15:10).

The same man, but a different "I am."

And Paul's letters are filled with new "I ams" that belong to every believer:

- *"I am crucified with Christ, and I no longer live, but Christ lives in me"* (Galatians 2:20).
- *"I am the righteousness of God in Christ"* (2 Corinthians 5:21).
- *"I am God's workmanship"* (Ephesians 2:10).
- *"I am more than a conqueror"* (Romans 8:37).

Watchman Nee wrote: *"Our old history ends with the cross; our new history begins with the resurrection."* (Nee, 1961) [15]

Kevin Rice expands this reality in *Cultivating the New Nature*: *"Just because we've been birthed into the family of God with His traits of righteousness encoded in our spiritual nature doesn't mean everything we do… is righteous. We must take ownership of our new nature and grow into the fullness of Christ."* (Rice, 2023a) [16]

---

[15] Watchman Nee, *The Normal Christian Life* (Wheaton: Tyndale House, 1961)
[16] Kevin Rice, *Cultivating the New Nature* (EKI Publishing, 2023

Your old "I am" dies at Calvary. Your new "I am" rises in the empty tomb. And now you must walk in it - own it - declare it until heaven's truth becomes your lived reality.

What Are You Saying?

So let me ask you: what are you saying over yourself?

Are you still whispering, *"I am unworthy. I am broken. I am beyond repair"?*

Or are you declaring what Heaven already speaks?

- *"I am a child of God"* (Romans 8:16).
- *"I am a new creation"* (2 Corinthians 5:17).
- *"I am more than a conqueror"* (Romans 8:37).
- *"I am unchained."*

Words are not decoration. They are direction.

When you confess false "I ams," you walk into chains. When you confess true "I ams," you step into freedom.

Proverbs 18:21 reminds us: *"Death and life are in the power of the tongue."* What you repeat becomes what you believe. What you believe becomes how you live.

Imagine waking up each morning and declaring:

"I am Spirit-born. I am loved. I am chosen. I am free. I am unchained."

How would that change the way you enter your workplace? How would that shape your relationships? How would that silence the accuser when he hisses, *"You are not enough"?*

Brennan Manning once said: *"Define yourself radically as one beloved by God. This is the true self. Every other identity is illusion."* (Manning, 1994) 17

Some people have asked me, *"But what if my I Am statements are a lie? What if I say, 'I am the righteousness of God,' but my behavior doesn't look righteous? Wouldn't that be sin?"*

Hear me: if your thinking, actions, behaviors, and habits do not yet match the Word of God, you don't change the Word to fit your life - you change your life to fit the Word.

The "I Am" statements drawn from Scripture are not lies. They are prophecies, invitations, and identities rooted in what Christ has already done. If your flesh tries to rise up against them, crucify it daily (Luke 9:23). If shame whispers, *"You are just a sinner saved by grace,"* recognize that for what it is - a lie. The sinner you were is dead. And to keep him dead, you must keep nailing him to the cross.

You are not resurrecting your old nature; you are stepping into your new nature. That is not dishonesty. That is discipleship.

The Sound of "I Am"

Declarations were never meant to echo in isolation. They were always meant to be spoken in the company of the redeemed. Heaven's language was never singular - it was *symphonic.*

---

17 Brennan Manning, *Abba's Child: The Cry of the Heart for Intimate Belonging* (Colorado Springs: NavPress, 1994)

When believers gather and declare identity aloud, something holy happens: the atmosphere begins to align with truth.

I've seen it - one trembling voice whispers, *"I am chosen,"* and the room answers back, *"Yes, you are."* Another lifts their head and says, *"I am free,"* and prayer rises like wind through the space. Another, barely audible, confesses, *"I am His,"* and suddenly the room feels like Heaven's porch - alive with belonging. That's not performance; it's formation. Each word becomes a hammer against invisible chains.

Declarations build culture. Culture shapes destiny.

The early believers understood this rhythm well. *"They devoted themselves to the apostles' teaching and to fellowship, to the breaking of bread and to prayer"* (Acts 2:42). Their identity was not declared in isolation but confirmed in communion - around Word, Table, and Body. Every "I am" found harmony in the "we are." In that fellowship, truth was tested, hearts were restored, and belonging became tangible. So do not declare alone. Let your confessions be shaped by Scripture, nourished in fellowship, and sealed in prayer. This is how declarations mature into culture and culture matures into Kingdom.

But not every declaration deserves agreement. The mouth can speak resurrection - or resurrect the wrong man. Paul warned us: *"The acts of the flesh are obvious..."* (Galatians 5:19-21). Jealousy, pride, impurity, rage - these are counterfeit "I ams." So weigh your words on Heaven's scale. Test them against the fruit of the Spirit (Galatians 5:22-23).

If your "I am" reflects love, joy, peace, patience, kindness, goodness, faithfulness, gentleness, or self-control - declare it boldly. If it echoes the flesh, crucify it. Don't decorate the old man with new language; let the Cross be your filter.

And do not declare alone. Scripture commands, *"Exhort one another daily, while it is called Today"* (Hebrews 3:13). Identity was never meant to be maintained in isolation but guarded in fellowship. We call truth out of each other until hearts grow tender again. That is the sound of revival in slow motion - disciples reminding disciples who they really are.

You are not "I am broken." You are "I am being made whole." You are not "I am forgotten." You are "I am found."

When a company of believers begins to speak that way, the earth itself listens. Because declarations are not just words - they are seeds. And the soil of culture is waiting for a people who will sow Heaven's vocabulary.

This is how a Kingdom sounds. Not illusions. Not labels. Declarations. Spoken in rhythm with the One who is, and was, and always will be - *I AM*.

.

Scripture Index

#IAmHis.

#SpiritBorn.

#Unchained.

Apostolic Equipping:

How to Form "I Am Circles"

Declarations are multiplied when practiced together. To establish an *"I Am Circle"*:

- Gather 3 - 5 trusted believers.
- Each person speaks one Spirit-born "I am" aloud.
- The group repeats it back, sealing it in agreement.
- End by praying these truths over one another.

This trains hearts not to echo the old man but to declare what God has raised. Over time, these circles become ecosystems of freedom, multiplying unchained identity across families and communities.

Chapter Five

Whose Am I?

The deeper question behind every identity crisis is not just *"Who am I?"* but *"Whose am I?"*

Because belonging defines identity. To know who you are, you must know whose you are.

A child knows whose name they carry.

A bride knows whose covenant she has entered.

A servant knows whose household he serves.

And you - you were never meant to drift nameless through life. You were meant to be claimed.

Chains of False Belonging and False Owners

But the world is full of false masters.

Sin whispers: *"You are mine."*

Shame hisses: *"You are mine."*

Addiction, fear, religion, culture - each tries to stamp its mark, to claim your allegiance, to own your story.

The enemy is a counterfeiter. He brands with lies: *"You are dirty. You are worthless. You are abandoned."*

These are not names. They are chains. Counterfeit seals meant to mark you as property of shame.

But no counterfeit stamp can outlast the seal of the Spirit.

The enemy knows your hunger for belonging and twists it into chains.

Some chain themselves to relationships that abuse them, hoping proximity equals love. Others tie their worth to crowds that cheer one day and curse the next. Still others mistake religious performance for belonging, thinking that if they work hard enough, maybe God will let them in.

But these are all counterfeits. They are not belonging; they are bondage.

The Body of Death

Paul's anguished cry in Romans 7:24 - *"Who will rescue me from this body of death?"* - echoed a punishment in the ancient world. In Etruscan and Roman practice, a murderer could be shackled to the corpse of his victim - face to face, limb to limb - until decay spread into his own body [Virgil, 1990] [18]. Virgil described how Mezentius bound "the living and the dead... face to face and hand to hand" until both perished [Brunschwig, 1986] [19].

This is what it is like to carry false belonging or to affirm the old man with your "I am." You are fastening yourself to decay. To keep wearing shame as identity is to drag a corpse on your

---

[18] Virgil, *The Aeneid*, trans. Robert Fitzgerald (New York: Vintage Classics, 1990).

[19] Jacques Brunschwig, *Ancient Roman Punishments* (Paris: CNRS, 1986).

back. Do not polish those chains and call them jewelry. Do not hang them around your neck and call them personality. The cross is not a decoration; it is execution. What it kills, Christ raises brand new.

Slaves and Sons

Paul wrote it clearly: *"The Spirit you received does not make you slaves, so that you live in fear again; rather, the Spirit you received brought about your adoption to sonship. And by Him we cry, 'Abba, Father.' The Spirit Himself testifies with our spirit that we are God's children"* (Romans 8:15-16).

Before Christ, we were slaves. Bound to sin. Owned by fear. Powerless to change masters.

But in Christ, the paperwork has changed. We are not just pardoned slaves. We are adopted children. Belonging is not a probation card; it is a birth certificate. It is not an allowance God grudgingly doles out; it is an inheritance He joyfully seals in blood.

Belonging answers the question, *Whose am I?* with Heaven's decree: *You are Mine.* And when you say *"I am His,"* remember: you are not echoing the condemned flesh. You are echoing the Spirit-born nature God raised from the grave. The old self is buried; what rises is holy, adopted, and filled with His breath.

Paul pressed it further: *"You are no longer a slave, but God's child; and since you are His child, God has made you also an heir"* (Galatians 4:7).

49

Your value is not measured by what you produce for your master. Your identity is secured by whose child you are.

Bought With a Price

Ownership comes at a cost.

Paul reminds us: *"You are not your own; you were bought with a price"* (1 Corinthians 6:19-20).

The blood of Jesus is not just pardon. It is purchase. The cross is the cosmic receipt that silences every rival claim.

When Jesus declared, *"It is finished"* (John 19:30), He was not only announcing the defeat of sin, but also your redemption. You changed hands. You moved households. You were transferred from darkness to light, from slavery to adoption (Colossians 1:13-14).

J.I. Packer said it best: *"Adoption is the highest privilege that the gospel offers: higher even than justification."* [Packer, 1973] [20] To be justified is to be declared innocent. But to be adopted is to be declared Mine.

Covenant Belonging

Hear His words in Isaiah: *"Do not fear, for I have redeemed you; I have called you by name, you are Mine"* (Isaiah 43:1).

This is covenant language. God is not making a suggestion; He is making a claim. He is saying: *"Your name is written into My story, sealed by My word, bound by My blood."*

---

[20] J.I. Packer, *Knowing God* (Downers Grove, IL: InterVarsity Press, 1973)

Hosea's marriage was a prophetic parable of this covenant. Even when his wife ran after other lovers, Hosea pursued her, bought her back, and said: *"You are to live with me, and I will be faithful to you"* (Hosea 3:3).

That is what belonging looks like. Not earned, but pursued. Not bargained, but bought. Not fragile, but covenant.

Metamorphosis of Belonging

If you are born again of the water and the Spirit, already, you are adopted. Already, the Spirit cries out within you. And yet, you are still learning to live as family, still growing into the culture of Heaven's house.

This is the metamorphosis of belonging: the seed is true the moment you are born again, but the branches stretch wider over a lifetime. You are fully His - yet still being fathered into maturity. The verdict is settled, but the vessel is still being shaped.

Belonging in Culture

Belonging is not just personal; it becomes cultural. A church, a family, a small group - each is called to be a household of belonging.

This is why Paul continually addressed believers as brothers, sisters, saints, and family. He wasn't building organizations; he was birthing households.

Cultural Application: Creating a Household of Belonging

Belonging becomes tangible through practice. Here are simple ways families and small groups can embody it:

- **Blessings at meals:** Speak identity over each person as food is shared.
- **Celebrate spiritual birthdays:** Mark the day of new birth like natural birthdays.
- **Shared confessions:** Declare together, *"We are His. Chosen. Spirit-born."*
- **Prophetic encouragement:** Set aside time to remind each other of Heaven's truth.

These practices make belonging visible. No one has to wonder *Whose am I?* when the answer is rehearsed in love, week after week.

But love cannot be allowed to calcify into empty tradition. When we trade living covenant for lifeless ritual, the fire goes out and only ashes remain. Tradition itself then becomes a chain - binding us to motions without meaning, forms without freedom. Keep the flame alive. Keep the chains falling. Let every practice of belonging stay fresh with breath from Heaven, so that meaning is not lost, and freedom is never forgotten.

The Seal of the Spirit

And God has not left His claim invisible. Paul tells us: *"When you believed, you were marked in Him with a seal, the promised Holy Spirit, who is a deposit guaranteeing our inheritance"* (Ephesians 1:13-14).

The Spirit is not a vague feeling. He is God's ownership mark. A down payment of glory. A reminder that you are already claimed, already His.

Henri Nouwen wrote: *"I am not what I do. I am not what I have. I am not what people say about me. I am the beloved of God. That is who I am. And that is whose I am."* (Nouwen, 1992) [21]

Kevin Rice expands in *Cultivating the New Nature*: *"Our spiritual man is reborn unto God's purpose… We must 'put on the new man' daily. As this new nature dominates, we'll be endued with power from on high."* (Rice, 2023a) [22]

Belonging is not a one-time ceremony. It is a daily confession. Each morning you put on the new man, each day you renew the mind, each breath you remind yourself: *I am His.*

The Shepherd's Voice

Jesus said: *"My sheep hear My voice, and I know them, and they follow Me… no one will snatch them out of My hand"* (John 10:27-28).

---

[21] Henri J.M. Nouwen, *Life of the Beloved* (New York: Crossroad Publishing, 1992)
[22] Kevin Rice, *Cultivating the New Nature* (EKI Publishing, 2023)

To belong to Him is to be held. It is to know that no matter how loud the voices of shame, no rival claim can pull you from His hand.

You are not just tolerated in His flock. You are named. Known. Carried.

A Story of Belonging

I know a man who could not escape the label *"failure."* Divorce branded him. Regret defined him. Shame claimed to own him. For years, he walked with bowed head, convinced he was little more than damaged property.

But one night in prayer, he whispered, *"God, I don't even know if You want me."*

And in that silence, he heard the whisper of belonging: *"You are Mine."*

It wasn't thunder. It wasn't a sermon. It was a Father's voice. And it broke chains that had bound him for decades.

That whisper still echoes today.

Are You His?

Every soul answers to a master. Paul wrote, *"You are slaves to the one you obey"* (Romans 6:16). The question has never been *"Am I owned?"* but *"By whom?"*

Sin once signed your name in its ledger. Shame once whispered that you were its property. Fear once convinced you

54

that you would never belong again. But redemption rewrote the deed. You were bought with blood with a price (1 Corinthians 6:20). Sealed with the Holy Spirit of promise (Ephesians 1:13). Transferred from the dominion of darkness into the kingdom of His beloved Son (Colossians 1:13-14).

You are not tolerated; you are treasured. The Lord your God rejoices over you with singing (Zephaniah 3:17). You are not on probation; you are in covenant. - His law written not on stone but on your heart (Hebrews 8:10).
You are not surviving your sentence; you are living your adoption (Romans 8:15-17)..

He didn't purchase you to employ you - He purchased you to embrace you. You are not a servant earning wages; you are a child inheriting promises (Galatians 4:7). And every rival claim has been voided by the voice that thundered from Calvary: *"It is finished."* (John 19:30)

So let the false owners be silenced. Let the old contracts burn. Let every chain that once defined you fall at His feet.

You are not sin's. You are not shame's. You are not the world's.

You are beloved. You are adopted. You are God's.

He holds your name in His covenant hands and says, *"Fear not, for I have redeemed you; I have called you by name, you are Mine."* (Isaiah 43:1). Not tolerated. Not temporary. Chosen.

So drop the corpse (Romans 6:6). Lay down the chains. Stand as family. And when the old masters call your name, let Heaven's truth answer louder:

"I am His. I am redeemed. I am unchained." (John 8:36)

Scripture Index

#IAmHis

#Redeemed

#Unchained

Apostolic Equipping:

How to Create a Household of Belonging

Belonging doesn't happen by accident - it is cultivated. If the chains of shame are forged in silence, then the chains of freedom are forged in sound: the words we speak, the blessings we rehearse, the identities we declare. These practices are not small gestures; they are kingdom rhythms that plant identity deep in the soul.

- At the dinner table, speak blessings of identity - let every meal become an altar where sons and daughters hear who they are.
- Celebrate spiritual birthdays as covenant markers - the days chains broke and new names were written in Heaven.
- Form group declarations: *"We are His. Chosen. Spirit-born. Unchained."* - rehearse Heaven's verdict until it drowns out the world's.
- Practice prophetic encouragement - speak God's truth until lies lose their power.

These rhythms turn families and fellowships into households of adoption, where no one doubts whose they are.

And remember this: if love is not rehearsed, fear will be. If identity is not spoken, shame will fill the silence. Households of belonging must choose their sound - the rattle of chains, or the echo of adoption.

Chapter Six

What Am I Worth?

The world is relentless in its demand for proof of your value.

What do you earn?

What have you achieved?

How well do you perform?

How flawless do you appear?

And yet beneath all those measurements lies the haunting ache every human heart eventually whispers:

What am I worth?

False Economies of Worth

We live in a marketplace of value where worth is reduced to digits and opinions. But these economies are counterfeit, designed to enslave rather than free.

The Israelites fell into this trap when they clamored for a king who looked impressive. Saul had stature, charisma, and approval. Yet his heart was hollow, and his reign spiraled into fear and insecurity.

God had already spoken: *"The Lord does not look at the things people look at. People look at the outward appearance, but the Lord looks at the heart"* (1 Samuel 16:7).

Human worth is fragile when it rests on what can be measured or applauded. Heaven's economy runs on a different scale.

Kingdom Economics:

In God's household, worth is never for hoarding or competing; it is for building. When you know you are priceless, you stop scrambling to prove yourself or to stockpile. You begin to steward resources and relationships for multiplication. Apostolic teaching always ties identity to stewardship - worth that is hoarded shrivels, but worth that is shared multiplies. When you know your worth, you stop hoarding or competing - you start building.

Bought With a Price

Paul reminds us with piercing clarity: *"You are not your own; you were bought with a price"* (1 Corinthians 6:19-20).

Worth is not a vague feeling. It is measurable by the most costly exchange in history: the blood of Jesus Christ.

When Jesus declared from the cross, *"It is finished"* (John 19:30), He wasn't just announcing the end of suffering. He was signing the cosmic receipt. The ransom was paid in full. The value of your life settled forever.

Peter echoes: *"You were redeemed… not with perishable things such as silver or gold, but with the precious blood of Christ, a lamb without blemish or defect"* (1 Peter 1:18-19).

Gold fades. Silver corrodes. Blood speaks forever.

Tim Keller explains it this way: *"The gospel is this: We are more sinful and flawed in ourselves than we ever dared believe, yet at the very same time, we are more loved and accepted in Jesus Christ than we ever dared hope."* (Keller, 2011) 23

Your worth is not determined by how flawlessly you perform, but by how completely you are loved.

Garden Value Restored

But redemption is more than a purchase. It is a restoration.

Kevin Rice writes in *Cultivating the New Nature*:

"Without God, we can't resurrect our garden nature. It takes a supernatural experience… God transfers His nature and the mind of Christ to our account. This new, spiritual nature will transform the corruption in our hearts." (Rice, 2023a)[24]

Worth is not just about the price that was paid. It is about the glory that was restored. You were not designed for chains -

---

[23] Timothy Keller, *The Meaning of Marriage* (New York: Dutton, 2011)
[24] Kevin Rice, *Cultivating the New Nature* (EKI Publishing, 2023)

you were designed for Eden. And when you are born again, that original garden nature is resurrected within you.

This is the metamorphosis of worth: already blood-bought, already restored, and yet still being re-trained to live as if priceless. The verdict is finished at the cross, but the vessel of your life is still being shaped into Eden's likeness.

Shame's Counterfeit Currency

But shame still hunts us. It hisses its verdicts in the dark: *"You are worthless. You are broken. You are unlovable."*

David Webb names it sharply in *Escape the Shame of Babylon*: *"Shame: Hell's favorite weapon. When shame becomes identity…"* (Webb, 2025b) [25]

Shame is a false currency, charging you debts Christ has already paid. It brands with counterfeit labels, bankrupting your soul of joy.

But hear this: shame does not get the last word. The cross does.

Henri Nouwen put it simply: *"I am not what I do. I am not what I have. I am not what people say about me. I am the beloved of God. That is who I am."* (Nouwen, 1992) [26]

---

[25] David Webb, *Escape the Shame of Babylon* (EKI Publishing, 2025).
[26] Henri J.M. Nouwen, *Life of the Beloved* (New York: Crossroad Publishing, 1992)

Identity Clarification:

When you say *"I am worthless,"* you are echoing the corpse of the old man. When you say *"I am beloved, I am blood-bought, I am Spirit-born,"* you are echoing the new creation. God does not affirm the old self; He buries it. What He raises is holy, priceless, and free.

A Man the World Undervalued

I know a man who once worked in a university as a medical researcher. His salary was lower than others with equal or even lesser responsibilities. When he asked why, he was told flatly: *"This is as much as we can pay you."*

He didn't argue. He believed his past had diminished his value. Even while studying toward advanced degrees, he kept silent, afraid to ask for help. Deep down he thought, *"I'm not worth the bother."*

But one day, a professor pulled him aside and said: *"You should stay in research. You have a gift many others do not have."*

That affirmation didn't raise his paycheck or erase his struggles, but it cracked a lie. For the first time in years, he realized he carried value others could see even when he couldn't.

And time proved it true. He went on to publish over eighty peer-reviewed articles in seventeen years. In one year alone, he produced more than the entire medical school faculty and research staff combined.

His employer undervalued him. His own perception diminished him. But God's design in him could not be silenced. His worth was not measured by salary - it was revealed by the fruit of a gift heaven had sown in him long before the world tried to discount him.

Jesus and the Broken Jar

Mary of Bethany also understood worth in a way others could not. She poured an alabaster jar of perfume - worth a year's wages - over Jesus' feet (John 12:3).

The disciples grumbled, *"Why this waste?"* But Jesus defended her: *"Leave her alone… what she has done is a beautiful thing to Me"* (Mark 14:6).

What the world called waste, heaven called worship.

This is the scandal of value: what seems foolish, extravagant, or wasted in earthly eyes is often priceless in heaven's gaze.

The Prodigal's Return

Another story: a young man rehearsed his confession. *"I am no longer worthy to be called your son; make me like one of your hired servants"* (Luke 15:19).

But the Father ran to meet him. He clothed him with a robe, slipped a ring on his finger, placed sandals on his feet, and ordered a feast.

The son measured his worth by failure. The Father measured it by family.

Sparrows and Lilies

Jesus Himself drew our attention to nature's simple parables of value:

"Are not two sparrows sold for a penny? Yet not one of them will fall to the ground outside your Father's care… so don't be afraid; you are worth more than many sparrows" (Matthew 10:29, Matthew 10:31).

And again: *"Consider the lilies of the field, how they grow. They do not labor or spin. Yet I tell you, not even Solomon in all his splendor was dressed like one of these. If that is how God clothes the grass of the field… will He not much more clothe you?"* (Matthew 6:28-30).

If He notices sparrows, He notices you. If He dresses lilies, He covers you. If He tends grass that burns tomorrow, how much more does He tend His beloved children?

A Modern Story

I know another man who once whispered through tears: *"I don't think I'm worth the breath it takes to pray."* Years of failure, addiction, and betrayal had hollowed him.

But one night he stumbled across these words: *"While we were still sinners, Christ died for us"* (Romans 5:8).

That verse broke him open. He realized the value of anything is measured by the price someone is willing to pay for it.

And if Christ thought he was worth His very life, then no failure, no addiction, no betrayal could ever reduce that value.

The Weight of Worth

Worth has never been measured in numbers. Heaven's scales don't read applause, salary, or approval ratings. They measure blood.

You were bought with a price - not with silver that tarnishes or gold that fades, but with the precious blood of Christ, the spotless Lamb (1 Corinthians 6:20; 1 Peter 1:18-19). That was Heaven's valuation of you.

From the beginning, God stamped His image into humanity's dust (Genesis 1:27). That design was never revoked; it was redeemed. What sin fractured, grace refashioned. What shame devalued, the cross restored.

You are not a salvage project. You are a masterpiece reclaimed. The world may auction worth to the highest bidder, but Heaven already paid full price.

Isaiah recorded God's decree: *"You are precious in My sight, and honored, and I love you"* (Isaiah 43:4). Shame calls you worthless; the Father calls you treasure. The nails didn't just pierce His hands - they pinned your price tag to eternity.

So let every false invoice be torn. Let every counterfeit currency lose its hold. You are not worthless. You are not disposable. You are not beyond repair.

You are blood-bought. You are Spirit-sealed (Ephesians 1:13). You are garden-restored. You are Heaven's inheritance (Ephesians 1:18).

The cross wasn't an act of pity - it was proof of priority. You were worth the sacrifice, and you are destined for the crown (James 1:12). The fragrance of your worship is not the smell of striving but of alabaster - broken, poured out, accepted (Mark 14:3-6).

So rise, son. Rise, daughter. Walk as one who knows the worth that cannot be revoked. Carry the weight of love nailed to the cross and sealed by the Spirit.

You are priceless. You are His. You are unchained.

#BloodBought

#GardenRestored

#Unchained

Apostolic Equipping:

Practicing Kingdom Economics

Kingdom economics is not about scarcity; it is about inheritance. The worth of a thing is measured by the price paid for it - and Christ has already paid the highest price for you. That value must be rehearsed until chains of competition and fear lose their grip.

- At meals, thank God not only for food but for the worth of each person at the table.
- In small groups, exchange affirmations: each person speaks one Spirit-born truth over another.
- Each week, release one resource (time, money, or skill) to bless someone else.
- Celebrate testimonies of restoration, so worth is rehearsed aloud in the community.

Kingdom economics trains us to stop hoarding, stop competing, and start building. In a world ruled by scarcity, the Church must echo abundance. In a culture bound by self-worth chains, sons and daughters must declare the worth Christ has already set.

Chapter Seven

Chains of Comparison

Comparison is a thief.

It sneaks in quietly - in classrooms, workplaces, sanctuaries - and it speaks in a small, steady voice: *"Look at them. Look at what you have not. Look at what you are not."* It dresses itself as information but leaves as accusation. It measures, it subtracts, it turns brothers into rivals and pews into proof of failure.

Paul warned, *"When they measure themselves by themselves and compare themselves with themselves, they are not wise"* (2 Corinthians 10:12). Comparison is a broken mirror; it never shows you the whole face.

The Garden Design

Comparison blinds us to design. It makes us envy another's fruit without noticing the roots God planted in us. Kevin Rice writes, "Our spiritual man is reborn unto God's purpose… We must 'put on the new man' daily. As this new nature dominates, we'll be endued with power from on high." (Rice, 2023a)[27]

---

[27]Kevin Rice, *Cultivating the New Nature* (EKI Publishing, 2023).

David Webb echoes this truth, reminding us that before we were formed, the story of our life was already written. (Webb, 2025c) [28] God's fingerprints were already impressed into our calling.

The question is not, *"Am I like them?"* but, *"Am I living from the new man I've been given?"* When comparison fades, purpose returns.

Identity Clarification: Every time you say *"I am"* you are either echoing the condemned voice of the old self, or the resurrected voice of your Spirit-born nature. God never affirms the corpse of the flesh - He buries it. What He raises is holy, beloved, and free.

A Dream at Fifteen - A Plan Without the Planner

When I was fifteen, the Lord gave me a dream. I saw a valley, dark and deep, with a ridge ahead glowing with light. Beyond it stood a multitude clothed in white, radiant, and strangely familiar. As I drew closer, I asked, *"Who are these people?"*

The Lord answered, *"These are the people your ministry will birth."*

I was young, zealous, and unprepared. I told my pastor what I had seen. He gave me a Thursday night youth service to preach. I stepped into the pulpit, hands clenched white against the

---

[28] David Webb, *The Unique Factor* (EKI Publishing, 2025)

wood, knees shaking, voice thin. I lasted five minutes before embarrassment sent me retreating.

Humiliation planted a seed, and I responded with resolve: *I will make a plan.*

Finish school.

Work my way through Bible college.

Pay every bill.

Map every step until I reach the dream's ridge.

The plan felt safe. It felt holy. But when the first year of Bible college collapsed under unpaid tuition and unanswered job applications, so did I. My pastor mocked my earlier words about revival. Shame wrapped around me like links in a chain. I believed I had failed God.

Years later, the Lord brought me back to that moment and whispered what I could not see then: *"I never asked you to make that plan. You left Me out of it. That is why I do not tell you every step. Because you would build ladders instead of trusting Me to lead you."*

That word cut me - but it also freed me. I realized comparison had chained me to other people's timelines, and control had chained me to my own. Destiny is not achieved through ladders. It is walked out in trust.

A Man Who Thought It Was Too Late

I know a man who once sat alone in his house, convinced that his timing was finished. Marked by his past, told by others he should disappear, he believed he had no hope for marriage, no chance for family, no path forward.

He even began to plan how to end his life in the least painful way for his parents. As he sat in that darkness, rehearsing how to remove himself from the world, his phone rang. A man he had only met once called, saying he felt God had told him to check on him. That unexpected interruption saved his life.

Today, every person he has ministered to is an indictment against the lie that he was finished. What looked like "too late" was not the end - it was the stage for God's redemption.

This is the danger of comparison and despair: it chains you to a body of death. But this is also the power of belonging and timing in God: one phone call, one whisper, one act of obedience can tear the shroud off the grave and remind you - you are not done.

Peter's Glance and the Better Mirror

Peter once asked about John, *"Lord, what about him?"* (John 21:21). The resurrected Christ answered him, *"What is that to you? You must follow Me"* (John 21:22).

It is the same correction He gave me years after my dream. Stop glancing. Stop measuring. Stop mapping ladders. What is that to you? You - follow Me.

Henri Nouwen once said that envy is the opposite of gratitude. (Nouwen, 1992) [29] It makes another's abundance feel like your poverty. Gratitude, however, restores your vision of God's unique design in you. Gratitude silences comparison's accusation.

Breaking the Ladder

Comparison is the quiet thief of calling. It doesn't shout; it whispers. It tells you someone else is further, better, holier - and you believe it until gratitude turns to grief.

But the Kingdom doesn't measure by ladders. Ladders are built by insecurity; altars are built by surrender. And the moment you start climbing, you lose sight of the Presence you were meant to walk beside.

Paul warned, *"When they measure themselves by one another and compare themselves with one another, they are without understanding."* (2 Corinthians 10:12) Comparison blinds the eye of the soul - it keeps you busy building instead of beholding.

Proverbs reminds us, *"Commit to the Lord whatever you do, and He will establish your plans."* (Proverbs 16:3) Ask before you build. Let Him critique the ladder before you climb it.

You are not called to outshine your brother; you are called to outlast your doubt. Faithfulness, not fame, is the measure of fruit. When you rehearse another's season, you neglect your own

---

[29] Henri J.M. Nouwen, *Life of the Beloved* (Crossroad, 1992)

soil. When you covet another's platform, you starve your own altar.

The Lord whispers even now: *"Be still, and know that I am God."* (Psalm 46:10) Not you. Not them. *I am.*

Your worth is not a race. Your timeline is not late. You are not behind - you are being refined.

So name your ache. Disappointment does not disqualify you. Grief is not condemnation. Let Him breathe on what feels buried. Let Him edit what you tried to engineer.

And when you declare, "I am," do not echo the corpse of the old man. Echo the resurrection of the new creation (2 Corinthians 5:17). Say it aloud if you must: "I am Spirit-born. I am enough. My time is now."

Because destiny is not found at the top of your ladder - it's found at the feet of your Savior. Gratitude is your breakthrough. Presence is your promotion. And trust is your crown.

So dismantle the ladders. Burn the blueprints. And walk again with the One who never measures, only molds.

You are Spirit-born. You are unchained.

Scripture Index

#SpiritBorn

#Unchained

Apostolic Equipping:

How to Call Someone Out of Comparison

Comparison shrinks culture; honor expands it. Culture shifts when believers live from inheritance, not insecurity. Start small - carry Heaven into ordinary spaces.

Today, practice Heaven's perspective:

- Refuse to measure yourself by anyone else - affirm your assignment.
- When a friend diminishes themselves, don't correct them with clichés. Call them out with gratitude.
- Speak genuine affirmation over someone others overlook.
- Say: *"I thank God for the grace on your life in…"* and name the gift you see.
- Gratitude breaks chains by reframing scarcity as abundance.
- Celebrate another's success as your family's victory.
- Replace envy with gratitude - thank God for diversity in His design.

When you lift others, the chain of comparison falls.

Freedom multiplies when identity becomes celebration, not competition.

Chapter Eight

The World's System

Whose system are you living under?

From birth, the world presses us into its mold. It teaches us to depend on performance, possessions, and popularity. It whispers:

- Prove yourself.

- Protect yourself.

- Promote yourself.

- Provide for yourself.

It rewards the strong, applauds the successful, and discards the weak. But beneath the applause and the production lies a deeper truth:

The world's system was never designed to give you life.

Dependence vs. Independence

In Eden, we were created to live in total dependence on God's Presence. Every breath was communion. Every need was supplied by His abundance.

But sin severed that dependence. Humanity chose independence. We built systems to replace His Presence, structures to secure survival without Him.

This is the essence of the world's system: man trying to be his own god.

Kevin Rice captures this in *The Noah Generation*:

"When man drifted from the Creator, he did not stop worshiping - he simply redirected it. The altars remained, but they burned to false gods, and man's identity was rewritten by the system he chose to serve." (Rice, 2023b) [30]

Worldliness is not just culture. It is a belief system. It teaches you to live as if God is unnecessary and to measure worth by what you can do apart from Him.

Babel: The Blueprint of Independence

At Babel, humanity conspired: *"Come, let us build ourselves a city, with a tower that reaches to the heavens, so that we may make a name for ourselves"* (Genesis 11:4).

It wasn't about bricks. It was about identity. Independence masquerading as progress. Babel was humanity's first attempt to create belonging without dependence on God - a culture built on comparison, competition, and control. But Heaven will not endorse what Hell inspires. God scattered them, because every

---

[30] Kevin Rice, *The Noah Generation* (EKI Publishing, 2023)

tower built on self eventually crumbles. Only what's born of surrender can stand eternal.

Egypt, Babylon, and the Names We Wear

The story of God's people is a story of chains. Israel groaned under Pharaoh's whips, Egypt's bricks, and the stench of bondage (Exodus 1:13-14). They prayed for freedom, but after generations in slavery, their minds were trained to submit. When Moses came with God's word of deliverance, they could barely believe; *cruel bondage had shortened their breath* (Exodus 6:9).

Israel knew these systems well. Egypt enslaved them with labor; Babylon exiled them through assimilation. Egypt's chains were forged by complacency - comfort disguised as blessing. They grew content to stay where provision once flowed. Babylon's chains were crafted from disobedience - a refusal to heed the voice that called them higher. One bound them by ease, the other by sin. And both still whisper today. Complacency and compromise will shackle any heart that forgets who it belongs to.

Babylon renamed Daniel and his friends (Daniel 1:6-7), trying to overwrite their covenant identity. That's what the world's system still does: it renames you until you forget who you are.

David Webb describes this in *Escape the Shame of Babylon*:

"Shame: Hell's favorite weapon. When shame becomes identity, it is not just bondage; it is Babylon." (Webb, 2025b) [31]

---

[31] David Webb, *Escape the Shame of Babylon* (EKI Publishing, 2024)

77

Slavery is not only ancient history - it lives among us. It hides in habits, masquerades as coping, and settles into identities we begin to defend. What Pharaoh did with whips and quotas, Babylon now does with screens, substances, shame, and applause. The form changes; the chain remains.

When you accept the world's names - failure, worthless, not enough - you live chained inside a false system.

The World's Arenas Today

This system still operates in our world. It's visible everywhere:

- **Money**: Where net worth is mistaken for self-worth.

- **Politics**: Where power is pursued at any cost.

- **Entertainment**: Where fame becomes an altar and applause the offering.

- **Religion**: Where performance and comparison replace grace and belonging.

These arenas are not neutral. They are systems that shape souls.

And here is the sobering truth: you can leave Babylon geographically but still carry Babylon internally. You can sit in a pew but still live as if applause, possessions, and performance define you.

The System Within

Kevin Rice writes in *Cultivating the New Nature*:

"Without God, we can't resurrect our garden nature. It takes a supernatural experience... God transfers His nature and the mind of Christ to our account. This new, spiritual nature will transform the corruption in our hearts." (Rice, 2023a) [32]

The enemy's greatest trick is not simply trapping us in worldly culture, but teaching us to carry worldly thinking inside redeemed hearts. Old systems of fear, self-protection, and striving cling like cobwebs.

To overcome the world, we must not only reject Babylon outside but crucify Babylon inside.

Chains That Still Hold

Slavery is not only ancient history - it lives among us.

I have had many friends I grew up with die from drugs and alcohol. Chains may change shape across centuries, but their grip has not loosened. What Pharaoh did with whips and bricks, addiction does with needles, bottles, pills, and glowing screens.

I think of one friend in particular. He was bound by drugs and pornography. He didn't know the Lord, but he came to a church service and was introduced to Jesus. To say his life was changed forever would not be an overstatement - and yet the chains of addiction still clung to him.

---

[32] Kevin Rice, *Cultivating the New Nature* (EKI Publishing, 2023)

He lived with a woman he wasn't married to. He nearly died when a drug deal went bad. Freedom was near, but slavery still stalked him. Eventually, he entered a Christian rehab program. And there, in a face-to-face encounter with Jesus - not just a fleeting feeling but a genuine encounter with the living Christ - his life was utterly changed.

He came home and burned every remnant of pornography and drug paraphernalia. He told his girlfriend, with whom he had a child, that he could no longer live outside of covenant. The very next Sunday, they stood in church and were married. She too had encountered the chain breaker while he was gone.

But here's the truth: the breaking of chains does not always feel immediate. Like an elephant trained from youth with a thin rope, we can grow strong enough to break free but remain conditioned to bondage. Even when the rope is no match for our strength, we stay tethered because we've believed the lie of bondage too long (John 8:36; Galatians 5:1).

That's what the enemy's system does - convinces you to stay when you're already free.

Witchcraft and Death Stories

I once knew a woman who lived among witches. Shadows were her companions, and familiar spirits wrapped themselves around her like a cloak. The air around her was thick - weighted with fear, control, and counterfeit power. One night she brushed against the Presence of God, and I saw her tremble as though the chains might split and fall. For a moment, she tasted freedom. But then she reached back for the darkness, stretching out her hands toward the very cords that strangled her. That is the cruelty of slavery - it whispers until the heart begins to love what kills it (2 Corinthians 4:4).

And I have watched chains cut life shorter than anyone expected. During a season of neighborhood outreach, we invited a man to church. He had never stepped into a church in his life. He promised he would come - he even laid out his clothes the night before, ready to walk through the doors. But before the dawn broke, his breath was gone. Our ministry team found him lifeless on his bed when they came to pick him up.

Another neighbor said she would come. She told her husband she felt a pull - an ache to return to church, the way she once went with her grandparents. Something in her life felt unfinished, hollow, missing its center. The church of her childhood had been wrapped in tradition, yet beneath its dust still burned a faint ember of power. That ember had marked her; it left a hunger that never stopped whispering. But she never arrived. A car accident silenced her before she could step into the freedom her heart had already begun to seek.

I will never forget those moments. They branded themselves upon me like fire: chains are not harmless trinkets. They are not jewelry to polish. They are not melodies to jingle as you walk. Chains devour. Chains cut short the music of a life before freedom ever has a chance to sing (James 4:14).

This is why the Scripture pleads: *"Now is the time of salvation"* (2 Corinthians 6:2). Not tomorrow. Not next week. Now. Every second, souls slip into eternity - souls Jesus already paid to redeem. We do not have a moment to waste polishing what Christ has already shattered.

I Know a Man...

I know a man who lived beneath the weight of this world's system. His worth was counted in promotions and paychecks. He worked late, built a gleaming résumé, and lived for the applause of strangers. But at home, silence grew where laughter once lived. His children stopped waiting at the window. His wife stopped asking when he'd return. He gave gifts instead of presence, money instead of affection. His body was weary; his soul was starving.

One night, staring at the ceiling in the blue light of exhaustion, he heard the Spirit whisper:

"What does it profit a man to gain the whole world and lose his soul?" (Mark 8:36).

He broke.

In that moment, he saw it - his own Babel, built brick by brick with pride and performance. And Babel had bankrupted him.

That man learned what every overcomer must: the world's system never plays fair. It promises freedom, but it was designed to enslave.

Jesus and the Kingdom Collision

When Satan offered Jesus the kingdoms of the world (Matthew 4:8-9), it was Babel's temptation all over again: independence, shortcuts, glory without the cross.

But Jesus refused: *"Worship the Lord your God, and serve Him only"* (Matthew 4:10).

Then Jesus stands up in Nazareth and reads Isaiah: *"He has sent Me to proclaim liberty to the captives… to set at liberty those who are oppressed"* (Luke 4:18). He doesn't offer a coping strategy; He brings a **Kingdom collision**. He disarms principalities (Colossians 2:15), crucifies the old master (Romans 6:6-7), and births a **new nature** in us by the Spirit (John 3:3 - 6). Our freedom is not self-help; it is **resurrection life**. (Austin-Sparks, 1950; Nee, 1961) [33] [34]

The Kingdom cannot be built on compromise.

The Church's Danger

David Webb warns in *Building the Kingdom in the Local Church*:

[33] T. Austin-Sparks, *The Centrality and Supremacy of the Lord Jesus Christ* (London: Witness and Testimony Publishers, 1950)
[34] Watchman Nee, *The Normal Christian Life* (Fort Washington, PA: Christian Literature Crusade, 1961)

"The danger is when the church itself begins to mirror the world's systems of power, control, and competition, rather than the Kingdom's values of service, humility, and love." (Webb, 2025a) [35]

A church that imitates Babylon may look strong, but it loses its soul. True Kingdom culture looks like washing feet, not chasing thrones.

The Kingdom Way

Tim Keller reminds us: *"The gospel is this: We are more sinful and flawed in ourselves than we ever dared believe, yet at the very same time, we are more loved and accepted in Jesus Christ than we ever dared hope."* (Keller, 2011) [36]

The world says: perform to belong.

The Kingdom says: you belong, therefore you live.

Henri Nouwen echoes: *"I am not what I do. I am not what I have. I am not what people say about me. I am the beloved of God. That is who I am."* (Nouwen, 1992) [37]

This is the only system that brings life.

Leaving Babylon Behind

Babylon has never needed chains of iron. Its strongest ropes are invisible - woven from fear, pride, and the desire to be

---

[35] David Webb, *Building the Kingdom in the Local Church* (EKI Publishing, 2025)
[36] Timothy Keller, *The Meaning of Marriage* (New York: Dutton, 2011)
[37] Henri J.M. Nouwen, *Life of the Beloved* (New York: Crossroad Publishing, 1992)

seen. It whispers, *"Prove yourself,"* until you mistake exhaustion for devotion. It teaches you to love the ropes that keep you bound, to call anxiety "ambition" and pride "purpose." But the Kingdom calls you higher.

Paul wrote, *"You were taught to put off your old self, which is being corrupted by deceitful desires, to be made new in the attitude of your mind, and to put on the new self, created to be like God."* (Ephesians 4:22-24) The first act of freedom is honesty - naming what Babylon has disguised.

John warned, *"Do not love the world or anything in the world."* (1 John 2:15) Love of the world is not affection - it's addiction. Babylon sells imitation identity: a cheaper version of sonship. But you were bought with a price far greater than its currencies of approval or applause (1 Corinthians 6:20).

Paul urged, *"Have nothing to do with the fruitless deeds of darkness, but rather expose them."* (Ephesians 5:11) To expose is not to shame - it's to bring light where darkness has claimed ownership. Freedom begins the moment you stop defending your ropes and start naming them.

Some of you still call your chains "personality." You say, *"That's just how I am."* But if it binds your growth, it is not personality - it is captivity dressed in charm. Christ didn't die to decorate your bondage; He died to destroy it.

Galatians declares, *"It is for freedom that Christ has set us free."* (Galatians 5:1) So stand firm. Don't let Babylon's lies redefine your worth. You are not a slave of Babel. You are a citizen of Zion. You are not renamed by the world. You are called by your true name - beloved.

The system you were rescued from is not your home. Its scales will never measure your value. Its towers will never reach Heaven. Babylon collapses under its own pride, but Zion rises through surrender.

So let the towers fall. Let the world's systems crumble beneath the weight of truth. Let every rope that once held your heart snap beneath the sound of your confession.

You are not Babylon's captive. You are not the echo of this world. You are not a slave to performance.

You are Spirit-born (John 3:6). You are garden-restored (Genesis 2:7; Revelation 22:1-2). You are beloved (Romans 8:15-16). You are unchained (John 8:36).

So rise, son. Rise, daughter. Walk out of the smoke of Babel and into the breath of the Kingdom. Your freedom is not rebellion - it's realignment. And every step away from Babylon is a step toward home.

Scripture Index

Apostolic Equipping: Recognizing Modern Slavery

Slavery today rarely wears chains. It looks like compulsions that shape culture - approval as currency, distraction as peace, pleasure as purpose. Babylon's ropes don't just bind; they train hearts to love captivity.

Apostolic communities expose these lies together and model a new rhythm - presence instead of performance, rest instead of striving, truth instead of image.

We don't modify behavior; we multiply freedom.

Kingdom Practices:

- **Name the Rope** - Confess what culture calls normal but Heaven calls bondage.
- **Exchange the Rhythm** - Replace busyness with stillness; replace scrolling with silence.
- **Create Culture Together** - Encourage one another daily; practice gratitude publicly.
- **Carry One Another** - Bear the burdens of your community until grace becomes instinct.

Step by step, we build a culture where confession replaces concealment and healing becomes normal.

The Chain-Breaker doesn't just snap ropes - He rewrites desires, retrains minds, and redefines freedom until Heaven's culture becomes ours.

(Galatians 6:1-2; Romans 12:2; Ephesians 4:22-24).

- Colossians 2:15

- Romans 6:6-7

- John 3:3-6

- Revelation 12:11

- Ephesians 5:11

- 1 John 2:15-17

#KingdomNotWorld

#SpiritBorn

#Unchained.

Chapter Nine

God's System

Every life runs on a system.

The world gives you one at birth: consume, compare, compete.

But heaven offers another: abide, believe, belong.

The question is urgent, piercing, unavoidable: **Which system rules you?**

The Passing Shadow of the World

John lays it bare: *"Do not love the world or anything in the world. If anyone loves the world, love for the Father is not in them. For everything in the world - the lust of the flesh, the lust of the eyes, and the pride of life - comes not from the Father but from the world. The world and its desires pass away, but whoever does the will of God lives forever"* (1 John 2:15-17).

The world's system is a marketplace of cravings:

- The lust of the flesh: addiction to pleasure.

- The lust of the eyes: obsession with possession.

- The pride of life: intoxication with power.

It is relativism dressed up as freedom, manipulation disguised as success, self-indulgence masquerading as joy.

But it is all sandcastles before the tide. *"The world and its desires pass away."*

A.W. Tozer warned: *"The world is perishing for lack of the knowledge of God, and the Church is famishing for want of His Presence."* (Tozer, 1948) [38]

The world's system cannot last. It enslaves. It devours. It vanishes.

Futility of the System

You can climb its ladders and still find emptiness at the top.

You can drink its pleasures and still thirst again.

You can grasp its power and still feel powerless in your soul.

It is endless striving. A treadmill to nowhere. A slavery disguised as freedom.

The Spirit whispers the warning: **The world's system cannot satisfy because it was never designed to give life.**

I remember as a teenager begging God for the Holy Ghost. I tarried at the altar night after night, waiting, watching others be filled while I stayed empty. Shame whispered, *"You're not good enough. It will never happen."*

---

[38] A.W. Tozer, *The Pursuit of God* (Camp Hill, PA: Christian Publications, 1948)

Then one night, when I was least expecting it, God poured His Spirit into me like fire and breath. I broke, I wept, I spoke in a new tongue. The waiting ended in breakthrough.

That night taught me something: transformation often feels delayed. You may think nothing is changing, that you are too stuck to grow. But God is working beneath the surface. What feels like futility is often preparation.

You Cannot Mix the Systems

Some try to blend the two. A little Babylon, a little Zion. A little pride, a little prayer. A little self, a little surrender.

But Jesus was clear: *"No one can serve two masters. Either you will hate the one and love the other, or you will be devoted to the one and despise the other"* (Matthew 6:24).

David Webb echoes in *Building the Kingdom in the Local Church*:

"The danger is when the church itself begins to mirror the world's systems of power, control, and competition, rather than the Kingdom's values of service, humility, and love." (Webb, 2025a) [39]

You cannot build Zion with Babylon's bricks.
You cannot walk in God's system while clinging to the world's scaffolding.

---

[39] David Webb, *Building the Kingdom in the Local Church* (EKI Publishing, 2025)

Mixture always collapses under the weight of glory; compromise cannot carry the Presence. Only purity can sustain the structure of revival.

God's Eternal Design

From Eden to Calvary, the story is not about systems but about fellowship.

Adam and Eve's independence shattered communion. Humanity built towers and empires to fill the void.

But in Christ, reconciliation has come: *"God was reconciling the world to Himself in Christ, not counting people's sins against them"* (2 Corinthians 5:19).

God's system begins here: restored relationship, unbroken fellowship, eternal belonging.

Henri Nouwen captured it: *"We are not loved because we can prove ourselves. We are loved because we are God's children."* (Nouwen, 1992) [40]

The world's love is conditional. God's love is covenant. The world's system fades. God's system endures forever.

A Kingdom Not of This World

Pilate asked about power. Jesus replied: *"My kingdom is not of this world"* (John 18:36).

---

[40] Henri J.M. Nouwen, *Life of the Beloved* (New York: Crossroad Publishing, 1992)

The world takes by force. God gives by grace.

The world enslaves with fear. God frees with love.

The world exalts self. God exalts the cross.

Earthly thrones rise through domination; Heaven's throne stands through sacrifice.

The kingdoms of men build walls of control; the Kingdom of God builds tables of communion.

The world demands recognition; Heaven delights in hidden obedience.

The world crowns the proud; God clothes the humble.

This Kingdom cannot be bought, bargained, or blended. It descends, not ascends. It conquers through surrender. And when it comes, every counterfeit kingdom trembles.

We are not spectators of this Kingdom; we are participants in its coming. Jesus didn't suggest we pray, *"Thy Kingdom come"* - He commanded it. Every time we pray those words, Heaven leans closer.

We're not asking for escape; we're asking for invasion - for God's rule to break into our ordinary ground. Each prayer, each act of mercy, each moment of surrender becomes an open door for His reign to manifest here and now.

Let Your Kingdom come - within us, among us, through us.

I Know a Man…

I know a man who once lived under the wrong system. His ministry became a scoreboard. Success was attendance. Value was offerings. Worth was measured by applause.

He built momentum, but not intimacy. He mastered growth, but forgot grace.

But in prayer, the Spirit whispered: *"Do not count chairs. Count hearts. Count tears. Count My Presence."*

It unraveled him. The applause grew faint; the Presence grew loud. He wept more than he spoke. He listened more than he led. Numbers no longer defined him. Presence did. The system shifted. Freedom came - and this time, it stayed.

Love as the Core

Paul defines the architecture of God's system in 1 Corinthians 13:

"Love is patient, love is kind. It does not envy, it does not boast, it is not proud. It does not dishonor others, it is not self-seeking, it is not easily angered, it keeps no record of wrongs. Love does not delight in evil but rejoices with the truth. It always protects, always trusts, always hopes, always perseveres. Love never fails" (1 Corinthians 13:4-8).

Every pillar of God's system is love. Every stone rests on Christ. Every breath flows with grace.

Brennan Manning said: *"Define yourself radically as one beloved by God. This is the true self. Every other identity is illusion."* (Manning, 1994) [41]

Until love becomes the lens, ministry becomes machinery.

Until love becomes the motive, service becomes performance.

Love is not an accessory; it is the essence. The Kingdom stands or falls on this foundation alone.

Transformation, Not Behavior Management

The world's system says: manage your image.
God's system says: be transformed by the renewing of your mind (Romans 12:2).

Kevin Rice, in *Cultivating the New Nature*, explains:

"Just because we've been birthed into the family of God with His traits of righteousness encoded in our spiritual nature doesn't mean everything we do… is righteous. We must take ownership of our new nature and grow into the fullness of Christ." (Rice, 2023a)[42]

God's system is not behavior management. It is metamorphosis. The Spirit doesn't polish the old self. He resurrects the new. He doesn't ask you to perform better - He invites you to *become* different.

---

[41] Brennan Manning, *Abba's Child* (Colorado Springs: NavPress, 1994)
[42] Kevin Rice, *Cultivating the New Nature* (EKI Publishing, 2023)

Religion reforms habits; resurrection reforms identity. Transformation begins where imitation ends. It is not about trying harder, but about yielding deeper - until the image of Christ becomes your instinct, and the nature of Heaven becomes your normal.

When the Church Reflects God's System

Imagine a community where no one performs to belong, where shame is silenced, where love is the law.

C.S. Lewis wrote: *"When I have learned to love God better than my earthly dearest, I shall love my earthly dearest better than I do now."* (Lewis, 1952) [43]

When the Church reflects God's system, heaven becomes visible.

Moses came down from the mountain, and his face glowed - he carried the atmosphere he had encountered. Peter walked the streets, and his very shadow healed the sick - he carried Presence that overflowed. Years later, when the old revivalist Billy Sunday came to town, taverns went dark and brothels closed their doors - not by legislation, but by transformation. Hearts turned, and culture followed.

This is what happens when love reigns. When the Church stops imitating the world and starts revealing Heaven, even cities

---

[43] C.S. Lewis, *Mere Christianity* (New York: HarperOne, 1952)

begin to breathe again. When we reflect His system, earth doesn't just look different - it feels different.

Heaven touches earth through faces that shine, shadows that heal, and hearts that love.

Living in God's System

Every system has a source. The world's system was built on pride, performance, and the illusion of control. God's system flows from love, grace, and surrender. The two can never be blended.

Jesus said, *"No one can serve two masters. Either he will hate the one and love the other, or he will be devoted to one and despise the other."* (Matthew 6:24) Babylon whispers, *"Do more, climb higher, prove yourself."* But the Kingdom whispers, *"Abide in Me."* (John 15:4)

One system builds towers; the other plants trees and cultivates orchards. One chases applause; the other cultivates peace. One shouts, *"Make a name for yourself!"*; the other says, *"Be still and know that I am God."* (Psalm 46:10)

Paul wrote, *"Do not conform to the pattern of this world, but be transformed by the renewing of your mind."* (Romans 12:2) That's the invitation - not to polish the old man, but to live as a new creation raised with Christ (2 Corinthians 5:17; Colossians 3:1). You are not a reformed sinner trying harder; you are a resurrected saint learning to breathe in a new atmosphere.

The world runs on scarcity. The Kingdom runs on sufficiency. The world says, *"Earn it."* Heaven says, *"It is finished."* (John 19:30)

When you live in God's system, you stop performing for worth and start producing from rest. You stop chasing ladders and start growing roots. Because love, not labor, sustains the soul.

Paul told the Corinthians, *"The old has gone, the new has come."* (2 Corinthians 5:17) This is the system of grace - reconciliation, restoration, renewal. You are no longer a product of the world's economy; you are fruit of Heaven's vine (John 15:5).

So let Babylon's scaffolding collapse. Let Babel's towers fall. Let every counterfeit crumble before the eternal.

You are not the world's captive. You are not bound to striving or shame. You are reconciled. You are restored. You are rooted in love (Ephesians 3:17-19).

This Kingdom cannot be shaken (Hebrews 12:28). This love cannot fail (1 Corinthians 13:8). This freedom cannot end (Galatians 5:1).

So rise and walk in God's system - where grace is the gravity, love is the law, and peace is the atmosphere. You belong to a Kingdom that will never pass away (Daniel 7:14). You are Spirit-born. You are unchained.

Scripture Index

#KingdomFirst
#SpiritBorn
#Unchained

Apostolic Equipping:

Discipling Someone Who Wants to Quit

Apostolic leadership isn't about pep talks. It's about Presence. When someone falters, don't shame them - stand beside them. When their faith wavers, lend them yours. When their hands hang down, lift them until they remember the strength still inside (Galatians 6:1-2).

Discipleship is proximity, not distance. It's listening more than correcting, believing for someone when they've forgotten how to believe.

Sometimes the greatest sermon isn't preached from a pulpit but whispered beside an altar, wept over a table, or written in prayer.

Kingdom Practices:
- **Stay Near** - Endurance is the language of love.
- **Speak Life** - Affirm what's resurrected, not what's broken.
- **Identify** – what needs crucified or should remain is buried,
- **Carry Together** - Pray and walk with them until breakthrough becomes shared testimony.
- **Model Hope** - Let endurance preach louder than advice.

This is how we disciple in a Kingdom culture - not to produce performers, but to raise sons and daughters who know how to rise again.

Chapter Ten

The Struggle is Real

The battle isn't always fought in fiery moments of obvious temptation. It is fought in the whispers of your mind. It is fought in the quiet tug-of-war of the heart. It is fought in the tension between who you once were and who you are now becoming.

And this truth must be faced head-on:

The struggle is real.

Faithfulness in leadership is not forged in stages or under spotlights. It is forged in hidden places where no one is clapping, where the work feels unnoticed, and where obedience is its own reward.

I still remember nights of exhaustion, crying in a church where the pews were empty and the grass outside was overgrown. I prayed, I polished, I labored, and I felt alone. And then the Lord reminded me: *faithfulness is never wasted.*

The Hidden Front Lines

We often picture spiritual warfare as angels clashing with demons in heavenly realms. And that is true. But most days, the battlefront is closer - it lives in our thoughts, our choices, our daily compromises.

Paul wrote with disarming honesty: *"I do not do the good I want to do, but the evil I do not want to do - this I keep on doing"* (Romans 7:19).

His words are not just his confession. They are ours. Sometimes it's subtle. You allow one movie with curse words, and before long you hear those same words slip out of your child's mouth. The compromise you tolerated has already multiplied.

Or it's a conversation with a coworker that shifts from innocent to flirtatious, replaying in your mind for days after. A night out with old drinking buddies seems harmless, but it drags you back into places you thought you'd outgrown.

Jesus lifted the standard when He said: *"Anyone who looks at a woman lustfully has already committed adultery with her in his heart"* (Matthew 5:28).

The world says: sin is only in the action.

Jesus says: the battle begins in the imagination.

We must learn to lead at the front line of our imaginations. Leadership is not easy. It never has been. Moses carried the complaints of a nation. David bore the weight of a crown too heavy for his head. Paul confessed to *"fighting without and fears within"* (2 Corinthians 7:5).

To lead is to feel stretched between vision and weakness. To be called higher while feeling lower. To shepherd others while fighting to stay whole yourself.

Faithfulness doesn't erase the struggle - it sanctifies it.

We must fight the good fight of faith on the front line of our imaginations in faithful humility, renewing our minds through the Spirit thus sanctifying our Spiritual man.

The Replay Loop

One of the cruelest parts of the struggle is not just the fall itself, but the replay that follows. The scene loops over and over in your mind. The words you shouldn't have said echo. The image you shouldn't have seen resurfaces. The opportunity you should have fled plays again, and again, and again.

Sin plants itself in memory. And unless the Spirit intervenes, memory becomes a chain. You can wake up free and still feel bound by what only exists in yesterday's echo.

But grace speaks into the loop.

The replay does not define you.

The Spirit is greater than the memory.

And sometimes, even faithfulness has its own loop. We measure leadership by visible success - attendance, applause, results we can count. But true faithfulness often looks like mowing a lawn no one thanks you for, or showing up to pray when no one notices.

It was in such moments - bent low over pews, tears mixing with polish - that I heard the Lord whisper, *"Faithfulness is never wasted, even when no one sees it."*

The enemy uses repetition to chain you to regret. God uses repetition to train you for endurance. One loop steals your strength; the other builds it. One drains your soul; the other shapes it into something unbreakable.

Let the Spirit rewrite the replay. Let grace turn your cycle of shame into a rhythm of faithfulness.

The Keeper of the Chains

An older minister once told me about his early years. He had felt the call to preach, but his pastor would not let him do anything except work the altar. Service after service, he prayed with the bound. He watched chains fall. He saw people leave free. Years passed before he was ever allowed to preach.

Looking back, he said those years at the altar prepared him more for pastoring than any microphone ever could. *"I was the keeper of the chains,"* he said. *"Not to put them back on people, not to label them, but to remember the power of God to set them free."*

He learned that the altar is Heaven's classroom - where compassion is forged, where authority is born, and where tears teach what titles never can.

Then he added a sobering truth: *"If you help free people from chains, you are walking in the heart of your heavenly Father. But if you place chains upon people, you are walking in the nature of the devil. Every chain you put on another becomes a link that binds you to your own judgment."*

Leadership begins in the altar - not with titles, but with tears. Not in striving, but in serving. Not behind a pulpit, but beside the broken.

Temptations Old and New

Temptation is not proof that you are failing. It is proof that you are alive in the Spirit - that something holy within you has begun to collide with what used to own you.

Kevin Rice writes in *Cultivating the New Nature*:

"Just because we've been birthed into the family of God with His traits of righteousness encoded in our spiritual nature doesn't mean everything we do... is righteous. We must take ownership of our new nature and grow into the fullness of Christ." (Rice, 2023a)[44]

The sharpness of the struggle comes from that collision: you are not who you were, but you are not yet fully who you will be. Temptation is the tension between death throes and birth pains.

And every generation faces this collision in new forms. The old temptations of the flesh still whisper, but the modern ones wear robes of influence and applause.

Every generation of leaders faces the temptation to confuse visibility with value. But leadership is not about a mic, a stage, or lights. It is about laying your life down so others can encounter the chain breaker.

---

[44] Kevin Rice, *Cultivating the New Nature* (EKI Publishing, 2021)

C.S. Lewis once warned that pride is *"the complete anti-God state of mind."* (Lewis, 1952)[45]

True leadership refuses to climb ladders of ego; it bends low to lift others. Temptation is not just the lure to sin - it is the invitation to self. And only crucified lives can carry resurrection power.

Against the Current

Before Christ, you floated with the world's current. There was no resistance, no struggle. The tide carried you wherever it pleased. But the moment you were born again - resurrected into your original design - everything changed. You were set against the flow.

Now the current pushes, and you feel the strain. That resistance is not a sign you are chained; it is the clearest evidence that you are free. The struggle itself is the proof of your deliverance.

David Webb writes in *Escape the Shame of Babylon*:

"Shame: Hell's favorite weapon. When shame becomes identity, it is not just bondage; it is Babylon. But those who know their true identity will not bow to its false verdicts." (Webb, 2025b) [46]

The very presence of struggle proves that you no longer belong to Babylon. You are swimming upstream in a world

---

[45] C.S. Lewis, *Mere Christianity* (New York: HarperOne, 1952)
[46] David Webb, *Escape the Shame of Babylon* (EKI Publishing, 2025)

content to drift toward destruction. Freedom is not the absence of pressure - it is the courage to resist it.

And this is where leadership begins. The way of Kingdom leadership runs against the current of culture. The world tells you to brand yourself, polish your image, broadcast your success. Jesus says, *"Whoever wants to be first must be last of all and servant of all"* (Mark 9:35).

Faithfulness doesn't always look like progress. Sometimes it looks like being found at the altar when everyone else has gone home. Sometimes it looks like carrying burdens no one else sees. Sometimes it looks like laboring in hidden fields where only the Father's eyes are watching.

The world calls that futility. Heaven calls it faith. You are not losing ground - you are building one. Each act of obedience is a stroke against the tide, each prayer a declaration that Babylon has no claim on you.

To go with the current is easy; to go against it is divine. Keep rowing. The river may resist you, but grace flows stronger still.

My Story of Ministry Struggle

I remember when my wife and I were planting a church. I was working a full-time job while pastoring, and every expense came out of our giving. Week after week, we handed out food baskets to families in need. For a while, they came. They sat in our pews. But as soon as life improved - a new job, a move, a change - they drifted away.

The church grew and shrank like the tide, and it wore on me. I knocked on doors, checked on members, only to hear again and again: *"Pastor, we found work. We have to move on."*

Many nights, I was alone at the church, polishing old wooden pews, tears falling as I prayed: *"God, why did You send me here to labor with no one to help?"*

One afternoon, as I knelt weeping at the altar, I heard the steady hum of a lawnmower outside. Curious, I went out and saw a man mowing the churchyard. He wasn't a member. He didn't even know I was the pastor. When I asked him why, he simply said: *"I'm just glad someone is using this place again. It sat empty for over a decade before you opened it."*

In that moment, the Spirit whispered louder than my tears: *"You are not alone. I see you. I am here."*

It was then I learned: faithfulness is never wasted.

That's the lesson of the struggle - it doesn't mean you've been abandoned. It means you're in the fight, and the God who called you has not left you.

The Soul Winner's Boot Camp

I also remember a weekend soul winner's boot camp I was asked to help with. I was the music, but I was also part of the team that led groups into the community to minister in the streets. Talk about intimidated.

I had pastored, preached, and played music for years, but I never felt adequate at any of it. And now, standing beside three seasoned leaders, I felt like an imposter just trying to keep up.

On the Thursday night of the event, we gathered for worship. During the service, a message in tongues came with interpretation. The Spirit broke loose. Afterward, we left the church on foot for a prayer march through the neighborhood. It was Halloween night.

We walked the streets, singing. We knocked on doors. We carried a trailer with a horse trough filled for baptisms. That night, more than sixty people were baptized and received the Holy Spirit. I was in awe. I felt unprepared, out of my depth - but God was undeniably moving.

By the end, people began to disperse back toward the church. Somehow, I ended up alone with the three leaders of the event. They didn't know the town, and they asked me to lead them back. I turned us toward an alley and said, "We can walk through here - it's only two blocks."

They froze. *"Is it safe?"* they asked.

I almost laughed. We had just seen chains of addiction shatter in the streets, watched the Spirit of God fall on dozens, and yet here they were afraid of a dark alley on Halloween night. I smiled and said, "Yes, it's safe."

As we walked, they began to talk about how it had been years since they'd been in a service where a message in tongues was followed by interpretation. I listened - and in that moment, something shifted. I realized these men were no different from me. They had doubts, fears, and shortcomings. Just because they carried a grace in one area did not mean they were invincible. We are all dependent upon the Lord for grace and increase.

Even now, I still battle feelings of inadequacy. I still carry shame for the mistakes I have made. But I know this: I would not be where I am today without the grace and mercy of God. And more than that, I've learned this truth: *my inadequacy is the very thing He wants to use.*

The hardest person I have ever had to lead is the man in the mirror - the one who thought he was disqualified.

Repentance: The Turning

The Greek word for repentance - *metanoia* - means *to change one's mind,* a complete turnaround. It is not groveling in shame. It is turning toward life. It is the sacred moment when drifting gives way to direction - when you stop floating with the current and begin walking against it in the Spirit's power.

Paul described it this way:

"Put off your old self, which is being corrupted by its deceitful desires... and put on the new self, created to be like God in true righteousness and holiness" (Ephesians 4:22 - 24).

Repentance is not a single act at an altar; it is a continual posture of the heart. Every day we turn. Every hour we realign. Every breath we choose again: *not my way, but Yours.*

And this is where true leadership begins. Not with perfection - but with repentance. David was not chosen because he was flawless. He was chosen because he knew how to fall. He knew how to break before the Lord and rise again in mercy's strength.

Brennan Manning once said, *"In love's service, only wounded soldiers can serve."* [2] Grace does not look for spotless hands   only surrendered ones. The ones who lead best are those who have limped through the valley and still lift their hands in worship. They know the sound of chains breaking, because they have heard their own fall.

Repentance is the rhythm of rebirth.

It is how kings are made.

It is how hearts stay free.

The Struggle Never Ends

Some believe that once you are born again, the battle ends. But Jesus never promised ease - He promised victory. He said, *"In this world you will have trouble. But take heart! I have overcome the world"* (John 16:33).

Struggle is not a sign you are failing; it is proof you are alive in Christ.

Before, you floated with the current of sin. Now, every current resists you. The friction you feel is not defeat - it is direction. The difference between bondage and freedom is not the absence of struggle, but the Presence of the Overcomer within it.

C.S. Lewis wrote, *"No man knows how bad he is until he has tried very hard to be good."* (Lewis, 1952)[47] The very pull you feel - the tension between what was and what is being made new - proves you are no longer dead in sin, but alive in Him.

And this struggle is not just personal; it is the forge of leadership.
Every calling stretches you between the *already* and the *not yet* - between the vision God showed you and the weakness that tries to silence it.

Kevin Rice reminds us: *"Our spiritual man is reborn unto God's purpose… We must 'put on the new man' daily. As this new nature dominates, we'll be endued with power from on high."* (Rice, 2023a) [48]

David Webb echoes the same truth in his quiet, steady way: *"Destiny is not the product of performance but of trust."* (Webb, 2025b) [49]

The leader's strength is not in perfection, but in perseverance. Apostolic faithfulness is born in the tension - the refusal to quit when everything inside you wants to. Chains are

---

[47] C.S. Lewis, *Mere Christianity* (New York: HarperOne, 1952)
[48] Kevin Rice, *Cultivating the New Nature* (EKI Publishing, 2023).
[49] David Webb, *Escape the Shame of Babylon* (EKI Publishing, 2025).

forged in complacency. Freedom is formed in resistance. The struggle is not your shame. It is your training ground.

Struggle and Spirit

Struggle does not mean you've been abandoned. Jesus promised: *"I will ask the Father, and He will give you another Helper, to be with you forever - the Spirit of truth"* (John 14:16-17). You are not left to fight alone. The same Spirit that hovered over the deep now hovers over the chaos in you.

The Helper indwells you. The Spirit equips you. The battle is real - but so is His Presence. He does not wait until your leadership is polished or your confidence returns. He steps into the cracks. He anoints the trembling. He strengthens hands that still shake and hearts that still doubt.

You may feel inadequate, but the Spirit is faithful in your insufficiency. Where you falter, He fills. Where you stutter, He speaks. Where you break, He breathes. Victory was never about your perfection - it was always about His presence.

Memory and Mercy

Struggles often resurrect memories. Shame loves to weaponize your past against your present, whispering the names of failures long buried. But Paul writes: *"Forgetting what is behind and straining toward what is ahead, I press on toward the goal"* (Philippians

3:13-14). Mercy outruns memory. *"There is now no condemnation for those who are in Christ Jesus"* (Romans 8:1).

Brennan Manning said it best: "Define yourself radically as one beloved by God. This is the true self. Every other identity is illusion." (Manning, 2005)[50]

Looking back, I see that mercy was already there - in the hidden places. In mowing the lawn no one thanked me for. In the quiet altars where tears fell like seed. In streets filled with the broken, where songs of deliverance rose from trembling lips. In alleys where fear and faith walked hand in hand.

Those were not wasted moments; they were classrooms of grace. They taught me that leadership is not forged in applause, but in anonymity. That mercy is not a reward for perfection, but a river that finds the lowest ground and fills it first.

So when memory speaks, let mercy answer louder. Your past is not a prophecy - it's the soil from which mercy blooms.

Five Marks of Apostolic Leadership

Leadership born in freedom and refined through tears carries a weight that titles can never grant. Here are five marks I have learned the hard way:

1. Faithful in hiddenness. Who you are when no one is watching is who you really are.

---

[50] Brennan Manning, *The Ragamuffin Gospel* (Multnomah, 2005)

2. Willing to serve before leading. If you cannot carry a broom, you cannot carry a mantle.

3. Equips others instead of hoarding authority. Apostolic leaders multiply freedom, not followers.

4. Lives under accountability. Chains break in community, not isolation.

5. Sees chains in others and helps break them. Authority is never about control; it is about release.

True leadership doesn't rise from ambition - it flows from the altar. It begins where pride dies, freedom breathes, and love takes command.

The Mirror Test

Leadership is not tested in the pulpit. It is tested at the mirror.

The man in the mirror knows your story. He knows your shame, your striving, your secret doubts. He remembers the nights you wanted to quit and the mornings you went through the motions anyway. He bears the hidden scars you pray no one ever notices.

But when the Spirit looks into that same mirror, He sees something different. He sees a son. He sees a daughter. He sees purpose wrapped in mercy. And His voice drowns out the accusations: *"You are Mine. You are my son. You are my daughter. You are chosen."* (Romans 8:15-16).

114

The enemy chains with accusation. God leads with adoption. One enslaves through memory; the other frees through identity. Every time you choose to believe what the Father says about you instead of what shame repeats, another link breaks.

True leadership begins when you stop hiding from the mirror and start reflecting the One who lives within it.

The Struggle and the Spirit

Every overcomer has a battle. Every saint bears a scar. The struggle is not proof of God's absence - it is evidence of His Presence at work.

Paul wrote, *"The flesh desires what is contrary to the Spirit, and the Spirit what is contrary to the flesh."* (Galatians 5:17) The fight inside you is not a sign of failure; it's proof that freedom is alive. Dead things don't wrestle - only the living do.

Your struggle is not your identity. Your identity is Christ. You are not condemned; you are beloved. (Romans 8:1) You are not trying to earn freedom; you are learning to walk in it. When the replay begins - the shame, the memory, the temptation - pause and declare, *"The Spirit in me is greater."* (1 John 4:4)

Victory is not absence of struggle; it is presence of grace. Grace does not excuse the fight - it empowers it. Paul begged for his thorn to be removed, but God answered, *"My grace is sufficient for you, for My power is made perfect in weakness."* (2 Corinthians 12:9)

That is the anthem of the unchained: weakness doesn't end the story - it reveals who carries it.

So lead the hardest person first - the one in the mirror. Lay down your ladders and titles. Be faithful in hidden places, where no one claps but Heaven takes notice. (Matthew 6:4) The secret battles of integrity are where crowns are forged.

Let shame's accusations be silenced. Let temptation's whispers be broken. Let mercy speak louder than memory. You are not chained by your battles - you are carried by your Beloved. (Song of Solomon 2:6)

The past may be loud, but the cross is louder. The struggle is real, but the Spirit is stronger. The fight is fierce, but grace is greater.

So rise, warrior of mercy. Struggle with hope. Fight with freedom. Press on with joy. Because every clash between flesh and Spirit is shaping you into the likeness of the Son (Romans 8:29). And every chain that once held you now rings as testimony - a song of broken metal, still echoing freedom.

You are Spirit-born. You are unchained.

Scripture Index

#StruggleIsReal

#SpiritBorn

#Unchained

Apostolic Equipping:

Leading Through the Struggle

The struggle is not the absence of God's call - it's the classroom of grace. Every leader meets the mirror before the microphone. The hidden wrestle shapes the public witness.

When shame whispers, let mercy speak louder. When failure repeats, remember: mercy does not run out.

The struggle does not disqualify you; it develops you.

Kingdom Practices:

- **Name the Battle Honestly** - Admit where you are fighting; honesty invites healing.
- **Let Mercy Define You** - Return to the altar until mercy becomes your instinct.
- **Disciple Through Presence** - Walk with the weary until strength returns to their voice.
- **Lead Yourself First** - Before leading others, submit your struggle to the Spirit.

Apostolic leaders don't hide their weakness; they redeem it. They turn wounds into wells and invite others to drink.

Every time you rise again, the culture of Heaven advances one step closer.

Chapter Eleven

A New Culture

Every kingdom carries a culture. Culture is more than music, art, or food. It is the soil you grow in, the air you breathe, the atmosphere that shapes who you are becoming.

The world's system may oppose God, yet the world itself is His good creation, still groaning toward redemption (Genesis 1; John 3:16; Colossians 1:15-20).

Two cultures breathe around you: the world's and the Kingdom's. And every soul must decide whose air it will inhale..

And the question is not optional: **Which culture is forming you?**

The World's Culture

The world's culture is a carefully packaged counterfeit. It wears the mask of freedom but breeds slavery.

It celebrates **relativism** - *"Your truth, my truth, every truth is valid."* It applauds **pluralism** - *"All roads lead somewhere; who are we to say which is right?"* It thrives on the **denial of absolutes**, insisting there is no final authority outside of man himself.

But make no mistake: the exaltation of man is the dethroning of God.

Paul writes: *"Do not conform to the pattern of this world, but be transformed by the renewing of your mind"* (Romans 12:2).

Culture is never neutral. It is either pressing you into the mold of the world or transforming you into the likeness of Christ.

The Kingdom's Culture

By contrast, the culture of the Kingdom is rooted in absolutes, saturated in love, and crowned by the glory of God. It bows to the Word, not to shifting opinion. It bends to the Spirit, not to man's applause.

Jesus declared: *"They are not of the world, even as I am not of it"* (John 17:16).

Kingdom culture is fruit-bearing culture. It produces lives that reflect heaven's atmosphere in the middle of earth's resistance.

Kingdom culture is not measured in numbers, budgets, or applause. It is measured in faithfulness.

Kevin Rice reminds us in *Cultivating the New Nature*: *"Our spiritual man is reborn unto God's purpose… We must 'put on the new man' daily. As this new nature dominates, we'll be endued with power from on high."* (Rice, 2023a) [51]

David Webb adds: *"Vision without obedience is just imagination. But vision shaped by obedience becomes destiny."* (Webb, 2025c) [52]

---

[51] Kevin Rice, *Cultivating the New Nature* (EKI Publishing, 2023).
[52] David Webb, *The Unique Factor* (EKI Publishing, 2025)

Kingdom culture is not a bunker. It is a catalyst.

The Sower's Warning

Jesus told a parable about seed and soil: *"A farmer went out to sow his seed. Some fell on the path, and the birds ate it up. Some fell on rocky places, where it sprang up quickly but withered in the sun. Some fell among thorns that choked the plants. Still other seed fell on good soil, where it produced a crop - a hundred, sixty, or thirty times what was sown"* (Matthew 13:3-8).

Here is the tragedy: many never fulfill their God-given plan because their soil never matures.

- Some allow the enemy to steal the seed before it can sprout.
- Some sprout quickly but collapse under pressure.
- Some let culture choke their destiny with distractions, wealth, or worry.

Only those who yield to transformation bear lasting fruit.

David Webb captures it in *The Unique Factor*:

"The difference between a life that withers and a life that multiplies is not chance. It is culture. What you cultivate daily will determine whether your faith shrivels in the heat or thrives in the harvest." (Webb, 2025c) [53]

Culture is not background. It is destiny.

---

[53] David Webb, *The Unique Factor* (EKI Publishing, 2024).

The Farmer's Truck - My Eyes Saw It

I once drove by an old farm where a rusted-out truck sat in the field. The paint had long since faded, the tire tread was worn, the bed eaten by years of weather. Most people would call it junk. But I saw something else: a relic of labor, a testimony to generations who had plowed and planted, sweated and harvested.

The truck was not beautiful. It was not shiny. But it told the truth. Its body was battered, but its heart still turned over. It could still move.

Faith is often like that truck. Not glamorous. Not pristine. Weathered, dented, sometimes nearly abandoned - yet still a testimony. Its usefulness is revealed in every bend, every scratch, every scar of service. Sometimes we polish and protect the very things we are meant to put to use.

I am reminded of another farm truck I once saw. I stood on the edge of a field where an old pickup sat frozen among the trees. The farmer had parked it in good condition - no dents, no breaks, its frame still whole. But time did what neglect always does. Seasons passed. Rust crept over the hood like moss, and the trees grew taller, their branches pressing in from every side. Roots twisted tight around the tires. Limbs swallowed the cab.

The truck could no longer be moved. It was boxed in, chained not by iron but by living growth. I could almost hear the faint rattle of old chains beneath the roots, a warning that neglect sounds like freedom until you try to move.

I saw it with my own eyes. I could go back today and lay my hand on the rust of that hood.

And in that moment, I understood the danger: even living things can bind what was once free. The very trees that began as shelter became bars. What was meant to shade ended up strangling.

So it is with the soul left untended. Good intentions, unpruned and undirected, become weeds that hold us fast. Growth without guidance becomes another chain.

But when the Spirit awakens, growth changes direction. It breaks outward instead of curling inward. It reaches toward light instead of wrapping around itself.

That is the difference between bondage and Kingdom life. One entangles. The other expands.

This is what Kingdom culture does: it grows in freedom until it overtakes.

Treasure in the Field

Another farmer, nearing death, told his sons, *"There is treasure hidden in the fields."* After he died, the sons dug furiously, turning the soil over and over in search of gold. They found none.

But the ground had been broken. The weeds were uprooted. The soil was rich with oxygen. And that year, their harvest was the best they had ever seen.

The treasure was not buried gold. The treasure was the harvest that came through cultivation.

Kingdom culture works the same way. The treasure of transformation is hidden in the discipline of daily digging. Prayer tills the soil. Worship uproots weeds. The Word turns over hardened ground. And the harvest comes - not by accident, but by cultivation.

Terraforming Culture

To terraform is to change an atmosphere until it sustains new life - what grace does in a heart, the Kingdom does in a culture. The call is not to survive within the world's culture but to transform it. To terraform the ground beneath your feet until heaven's atmosphere fills it.

Kevin Rice writes in *The Noah Generation*:

"The sons of God were not called to adapt to the world's atmosphere but to establish God's. They terraform the culture around them into the likeness of heaven." (Rice, 2023b) [54]

This is not withdrawal. It is invasion. The yeast working through the dough (Matthew 13:33). The salt permeating the meat (Matthew 5:13). The light scattering the darkness (Matthew 5:14).

Kingdom culture is not a **safe-space** - it's a wildfire of grace that changes the oxygen wherever it burns. It doesn't retreat

---

[54] Kevin Rice, *The Noah Generation* (EKI Publishing, 2023)

from corruption; it reclaims the soil. When Heaven's atmosphere fills a place, even the desert begins to bloom.

I Learned This the Hard Way

When I pastored in a small community, I often felt like I was sowing into barren ground. Families came, families left. Growth looked more like a revolving door than a harvest field.

I have to confess: there were days I almost gave up believing God could use me at all. Faith did not feel comforting in those moments - it felt cruel. I wanted to lay it down, to stop sowing into ground that looked barren. Shame whispered, *"You were never called."* Despair muttered, *"Your story is finished."*

My prayers felt like seeds thrown on concrete. My faith felt deaf. Yet heaven was listening.

I cried over those pews, asking God, *"Why sow here if no fruit remains?"*

And He whispered: *"You are not only sowing into people; you are sowing into culture. You are preparing a harvest you may not yet see."*

That is the hope of Kingdom culture: even when the fruit seems delayed, the soil is shifting. The ground is being terraformed. Heaven is breaking in.

Faith & Vision

Faith is more than sight. Vision is more than goals. Together they form the lens through which we see God, ourselves, and the world. But what happens when faith feels like blindness and vision feels like fantasy? When the promise seems delayed and the path disappears beneath your feet?

Scripture calls faith "the substance of things hoped for, the evidence of things not seen" (Hebrews 11:1). Faith isn't a reaction to what's visible - it's the proof of what's invisible. It's the confidence that God is moving even when nothing else is. The Lord once whispered to me, *"If you can see it, what use do you have for faith?"*

Faith begins where sight ends. It builds what eyes can't yet confirm and holds what hands can't yet touch. Vision isn't fantasy - it's Heaven's preview shown to a heart still walking through process. God trains sight in the dark so that trust becomes your true vision.

Oswald Chambers once wrote, *"Faith never knows where it is being led, but it loves and knows the One who is leading."* (Chambers, 1935) [55]

Faith is not blindness; it's divine perspective. It calls the unseen real because it trusts the unseen God. Vision without faith drifts into fantasy; faith without vision settles into survival. Together, they form the engine of perseverance - the holy stubbornness that keeps building when logic says stop, and keeps believing when evidence says quit.

Faith doesn't ignore reality - it invites Heaven to rewrite it.

---

[55] Oswald Chambers, *My Utmost for His Highest* (Dodd, Mead, 1935)

When you can't see the way forward, that's not failure - it's invitation. He's teaching you to navigate by Presence, not by proof.

Sight vs. Vision

Sight sees the rust. Vision sees the testimony. Sight sees the empty pews. Vision sees the harvest. Sight sees weakness. Vision sees grace. Sight measures the moment. Vision remembers the promise. Sight counts what is missing. Vision calls what is coming.

Paul wrote: *"We live by faith, not by sight."* (2 Corinthians 5:7)

Faith is not naïve optimism; it is sight baptized in trust. It doesn't ignore reality - it interprets it through redemption. Sight looks at what's dying; vision sees what's being born. Sight says, "Not enough." Vision says, "God is still enough." Sight stops at the obstacle. Vision walks through it. Sight sees giants. Vision sees covenant.

Faith is Heaven's corrective lens - it trains the heart to see beyond the visible and to build what isn't yet built. When sight stops, vision begins. And where vision endures, the impossible becomes inevitable.

What Kingdom Culture Looks Like

Kingdom culture is what happens when Heaven's essence fills human hearts. It is not learned behavior but **divine nature** awakened (2 Peter 1:3 - 4). It does not begin with effort; it begins with **new birth** (John 3:5 - 6).

The values of Heaven are not external rules to imitate but **internal realities written by the Creator Himself** - laws of love inscribed on living hearts, not tablets of stone (Jeremiah 31:33; 2 Corinthians 3:3). They are the atmosphere of those who **live and move and have their being in Him** (Acts 17:28).

Kingdom culture is visible. It is not theory; it is fruit (Matthew 7:16-18).

- **Love where hatred once ruled** (John 13:34-35; Romans 12:21).
- **Forgiveness in the face of betrayal** (Luke 23:34; Colossians 3:13).
- **Generosity in a world obsessed with consumption** (Acts 2:44-45; 2 Corinthians 9:7-8).
- **Joy that outlasts disappointment** (John 16:22; Habakkuk 3:17-18).
- **Holiness that will not bow to compromise** (1 Peter 1:15-16; Romans 12:2).

Kingdom culture is **Heaven made tangible - God's heart expressed through human hands** (Matthew 6:10; Philippians 2:13). It is not someday; it is here and now (Luke 17:21). And every time love overcomes fear (1 John 4:18), grace replaces judgment (James 2:13), or truth stands in the dark (John 1:5), the soil of earth begins to yield again to its original design (Genesis

1:28; Isaiah 51:3). Creation itself leans forward in expectation, longing for the sons and daughters of God to be revealed (Romans 8:19-21). Each act of redemption tills the ground for Eden's return - the restoration of Heaven's rule and realm upon the earth (Matthew 6:10; Revelation 21:1-5).

External Voices

Henri Nouwen once wrote, *"We are called to convert our restless hearts into a space where God can dwell."* (Nouwen, 1981a)[56] He also reminded us, *"The spiritual life does not remove us from the world but leads us deeper into it."* (Nouwen, 1974) [57] That is the essence of Kingdom culture - it doesn't retreat from darkness; it redeems it. The spiritual life is not an exit strategy but an invasion of grace. Heaven doesn't hover above the world; it inhabits it through sons and daughters who carry Presence into ordinary places.

A.W. Tozer warned, *"The church that can't say no to the world will never say yes to the Spirit."* (Tozer, 1960) [58] You cannot blend the two. Culture always demands allegiance. But when allegiance belongs to Heaven, culture begins to shift. We engage without compromise, influence without imitation, and love without losing identity.

---

[56] Henri J.M. Nouwen, *Making All Things New: An Invitation to the Spiritual Life* (San Francisco: HarperOne, 1981)
[57] Henri J.M. Nouwen, *Out of Solitude: Three Meditations on the Christian Life* (Notre Dame, IN: Ave Maria Press, 1974)
[58] A.W. Tozer, *Of God and Men* (Camp Hill, PA: Christian Publications, 1960)

A.W. Tozer warned, *"It is altogether possible to have religious activity without spiritual life."* (Tozer, 1955) [59] He later wrote, *"The true Church has never sounded out public expectations before launching her mission. Her leaders heard from God, they knew their course, and they moved forward."* (Tozer, 1955) [60] Culture always demands allegiance, but Kingdom allegiance belongs to Heaven alone.

As Tozer declared, *"We must make our choice between the synthetic faith of the world and the true faith that stands in the power of the Spirit."* (Tozer, 1955)[61] Kingdom culture is not escape - it's engagement. It enters the world not to copy it, but to convert it.

Kingdom culture isn't shaped by avoidance - it's revealed through engagement that looks like Jesus: holy, humble, and unafraid to touch what others avoid.

Living in a New Culture

Culture is not neutral - it is soil. Whatever grows in it shapes what breathes from it. The world's soil breeds striving, scarcity, and self-preservation. But Kingdom soil births faith, peace, and fruit that remains (John 15:16).

Paul pleaded, *"Do not be conformed to this world, but be transformed by the renewing of your mind."* (Romans 12:2) That word *conformed* means "pressed into a mold." The world loves molds -

---

[59] A.W. Tozer, *The Root of the Righteous* (Chicago: Moody Publishers, 1955)
[60] A.W. Tozer, *The Root of the Righteous* (Chicago: Moody Publishers, 1955)
[61] Ibid., 88.

systems that shape everyone the same. But the Spirit loves seeds - unique, alive, carrying the DNA of heaven.

You were never meant to fit a mold; you were meant to cultivate an atmosphere. Every act of faith is a seed. Every word of truth shifts the air. very declaration terraform's the ground beneath your feet until heaven's climate takes root in earth's crust.

Jesus said, *"The Kingdom of Heaven is like yeast that a woman took and mixed into about sixty pounds of flour until it worked through all the dough."* (Matthew 13:33) That is Kingdom culture - quiet invasion. Unseen, yet unstoppable. Heaven is not waiting for permission to arrive; it's waiting for vessels who will carry its air.

When gratitude replaces comparison, the Kingdom breaks through. When generosity uproots greed, the soil begins to heal. When rest dethrones busyness, heaven finds habitation.

Paul called believers "ambassadors for Christ" (2 Corinthians 5:20). Ambassadors do not adopt the culture of the nation they visit; they represent the one they came from. You are heaven's diplomat on foreign soil - a carrier of divine policy, sent to rewrite the atmosphere around you.

You are not conformed to this age (Romans 12:2). You are transformed by the Spirit (2 Corinthians 3:18). You are soil prepared for Kingdom seed (Luke 8:15). You are a living temple, hosting heaven's air on earthly ground (1 Corinthians 3:16).

So let Babylon's noise be silenced. Let world culture lose its grip. Let gratitude be your language, peace your posture, and love your law. You are not surviving culture - you are reforming it. You are not escaping the world - you are redeeming it, one breath, one act, one seed at a time. You are the culture of heaven on earth.

Scripture Index

#NewCulture

#SpiritBorn

#Unchained

Apostolic Equipping:

Cultivating Kingdom Culture

Apostolic equipping begins with cultivation, not control. We are gardeners, not gatekeepers. Kingdom culture doesn't spread by enforcing walls, but by planting seeds of grace in barren ground.

Culture shifts when faith becomes presence - when we sit beside the fainthearted until hope takes root again. Apostolic leaders don't just cast vision; they carry people through the in-between. They pull weeds, plant truth, and water dry soil with patience until heaven's atmosphere fills the field.

Transformation happens through proximity - discipleship in the dust, not distance from it. When others faint, stay close. When culture resists, keep planting.

Kingdom Practices:
- Look for small "fields" around you to cultivate - a home, a workplace, a community.
- Walk beside the weary; let your presence preach hope.
- Celebrate growth before harvest; heaven calls sprouting holy.

(Galatians 6:9) - *"Let us not grow weary in doing good, for in due season we shall reap if we do not lose heart."*

Chapter Twelve

Faith Over Feelings

Have you ever been handed a task that felt beyond your expertise? Maybe it was raising children when you still felt like one yourself. Maybe it was navigating marriage, or managing money, or standing at the edge of a brand-new calling.

Life doesn't offer preschool. You are thrown straight into the classroom of existence, and you learn as you go.

The same is true in the Spirit. When you are born again, you are not placed in a safe sandbox with padded walls. You are placed in the middle of a battlefield where flesh and Spirit wrestle daily (Galatians 5:17). And in that clash, feelings often scream louder than faith. Doubt demands evidence. Fear asks for guarantees. But Heaven only hands out invitations.

Here is the unshakable truth: **The most critical step in being an overcomer is beginning.**

Avoidance does not prevent defeat. It guarantees it. To overcome, you must "come over" something. And to come over, you must begin. Faith never feels ready, but it moves anyway. You cannot win a race you never step into (Hebrews 12:1-2).

Every stride of obedience becomes a declaration: *I was made for more than hesitation.*

Henri Nouwen once wrote, *"The spiritual life does not remove us from the world but leads us deeper into it."* (Nouwen, 1992)[62] Faith doesn't bypass the storm; it finds Christ in the middle of it. To begin doesn't mean escape - it means engagement, rooted and anchored in Presence.

Feelings as Indicators, Not Drivers

Emotions are real. They matter. They give voice to what's happening in the soul. But they are gauges, not engines. They testify, but they cannot drive.

Faith is not the denial of emotion - it is the enthronement of Christ above emotion. David wrestled with this tension when he cried, *"Why are you cast down, O my soul? Hope in God"* (Psalm 42:5). His feelings shouted despair, but his faith shouted louder.

A.W. Tozer called it *"the gaze of a soul upon a saving God."* (Tozer, 1948) [63] Faith always begins with a gaze - lifting your eyes above your feelings to His face until perspective shifts and peace returns.

You are not what you feel; you are what He declares (John 8:36; 2 Corinthians 5:17). Yet don't mistake restraint for expression. Faith doesn't silence emotion - it sanctifies it. Jesus wept (John 11:35). He rejoiced (Luke 10:21). He was **moved with**

[62] Henri J.M. Nouwen, *Life of the Beloved* (New York: Crossroad, 1992)
[63] A.W. Tozer, *The Pursuit of God* (Chicago: Moody Publishers, 1948)

compassion and healed the sick (Matthew 14:14). Emotion under His rule becomes fuel for mercy, not manipulation.

Dallas Willard once said, "Feelings make excellent servants but terrible masters." (Willard, 2002) [64] The Spirit doesn't silence emotion; He seats it in its rightful place - under love, under truth, under the Lordship of Christ.

So feel deeply, but follow divinely. Let emotions serve as indicators, not dictators. Let them bow to the King who felt perfectly - and still chose purpose over pain. Faith may not always feel right, but it will always lead right.

Elijah at the Broom Tree

Elijah had Mount Carmel days and broom-tree days. He saw fire fall from Heaven (1 Kings 18), and he also prayed to die beneath a desert shrub (1 Kings 19:3-5). The same voice that called down fire now whispered exhaustion. But God did not condemn him for feelings of collapse. He fed him, gave him rest, and then spoke in a whisper.

Faith does not erase human fragility - it carries you through it. Feelings say, *"I can't go on."* Faith replies, *"You are not finished yet. Eat. Rest. Listen."* (1 Kings 19:7-8).

And when Elijah felt utterly alone, God reminded him of a remnant - seven thousand who had not bowed to Baal (1 Kings

---

[64] Dallas Willard, *Renovation of the Heart: Putting on the Character of Christ* (Colorado Springs, CO: NavPress, 2002)

19:18). Even prophets need perspective. Even warriors need community.

Isolation magnifies despair; connection restores vision. God's answer to burnout was not rebuke, but nourishment and reminder: *You are not alone.* The whisper that revived Elijah still speaks today - not to the noise, but to the weary heart that listens.

When Beginning Feels Impossible

Peter walked on water because he began (Matthew 14:29). He sank when his feelings took over (Matthew 14:30). Yet the hand of Jesus reached down **immediately** (Matthew 14:31).

Faith is beginning again even after sinking. Faith is taking the first step even when your legs still shake. Faith is starting when feelings scream, *"Stay safe."*

Peter's story isn't about failure - it's about focus. He didn't sink because he left the boat; he sank because he looked away. And by the time the water swallowed his courage, he was too far from the boat for anyone else to save him. The other disciples could only watch. That's what faith does - it carries you beyond human rescue, into the realm where only God's hand can hold you.

The waves were real, the fear was real, but so was the hand that never let him drown. Every step toward Jesus begins with leaving the safety of the boat. Obedience often feels like risk until you realize it's rescue.

Faith isn't the absence of fear; it's the decision to move anyway. The miracle didn't happen in the plan - it happened in the motion. Heaven meets movers, not watchers.

When beginning feels impossible, remember: Jesus doesn't wait on the other side of your courage. He meets you in the middle of it.

Barbecue Smoke and Baby Saints

When we planted a daughter work eighteen miles from our primary church, more than twenty-six people were baptized and filled with the Holy Ghost in a single month.

These were brand-new believers - men and women who had never set foot in a church before. In the weeks following, they constantly invited my family to cookouts and barbecues. Eventually, I asked them, *"Why do you always want us around?"*

Their answer broke me. *"Since we were born again, we lost all our old friends. You are the only family we have."*

Somewhere between the laughter and the ribs, the barbecue smoke became holy smoke. In the same way Samuel's sacrifices filled the air with the aroma of worship, our little backyard grills became altars of belonging. What began as ordinary fellowship became sacred communion (1 Samuel 9:12-13; 1 Samuel 16:2-5).

It was in those moments I realized: the Church is not built by sermons alone - it's built by shared tables, by presence, by love that lingers after the coals die down (Acts 2:46).

It hit me in the ordinary places: on Friday nights when their phones stayed silent; on birthdays when no one from the old life called; at the end of workdays when the invitations to the bar stopped coming and were replaced by a hollow quiet. Conversion didn't just change their eternity; it changed their contacts, their calendars, and their table. The laughter they once knew was now mixed with awkward new silence. Old group chats went dead. New rhythms had not yet formed. The cost of discipleship was not just "repent and be baptized"; it was "lose the circle you once called home," and wait for a new family to gather around you (John 14:18).

Faith births belonging, but if the church does not embrace the newborn, they remain vulnerable, orphaned (Galatians 6:2).

Chains of sin had fallen, but chains of isolation threatened to take their place. And God whispered to me: *"You cannot leave My newborns alone. Be father. Be family."* (1 Thessalonians 2:7-8)

Since then, I have carried this conviction: **soul winning does not end at the altar; it begins there.**

The Treasure in Beginning

Jesus said the Kingdom is like seed planted in soil (Matthew 13:3-9). If you never plant, you never reap. The treasure of harvest is hidden in the act of beginning - of digging, sowing, watering, and waiting.

Every breakthrough begins buried. Seeds don't shout when they're planted; they die quietly before they rise. Faith is daily beginning, not occasional inspiration. It's showing up to water ground that hasn't yet moved. It's trusting that hidden work is still holy work.

Faith starts again tomorrow when today's ground feels hard. Faith refuses to measure fruit before the seed has taken root. Solomon wrote, *"Cast your bread upon the waters, for you will find it after many days"* (Ecclesiastes 11:1). Even when your obedience feels like it's floating away, Heaven has already marked the current of its return.

Heaven calls the act of starting sacred because it mirrors creation itself - God speaking light into darkness, calling life from what looks empty.

Begin again.

Because every act of obedience buries a promise, and every promise planted in faith will bloom in its appointed time (Galatians 6:9; Isaiah 55:10-11).

When the Heart Accuses

Your heart will condemn you (1 John 3:20). Feelings will rise like weeds, whispering, *"You're not enough. You can't change. Why even start?"* The mind becomes a courtroom, and the voice of shame takes the judge's seat.

But Scripture answers: *"God is greater than our heart, and He knows everything."* (1 John 3:20) He knows your failures and still calls you His own. He knows your weakness and still chooses you for His work.

Faith isn't pretending the verdict never came - it's letting God overrule it. Grace walks into the courtroom and silences every accusation.

To overcome, you must begin even when your heart screams you cannot. You must step forward, not because you feel ready, but because He is already there (Exodus 33:14; Romans 8:1).

Every step of obedience declares, *"My Judge has spoken. My case is closed."* Condemnation may echo, but it has no authority in the presence of mercy.

As David Webb reminds us, *"The Christian walk is not maintained by accident but by daily choices that confirm your true identity."* (Webb, 2025b)[65] Every time you choose truth over accusation, you strengthen the culture of Heaven within you.

Gethsemane: Beginning in Surrender

Jesus Himself knelt under the oil press of Gethsemane (Matthew 26:39). His soul was overwhelmed (Matthew 26:38). His

---

[65] David Webb, *Escape from the Shame of Babylon* (EKI Publishing, 2025)

feelings were raw. The weight of the world pressed against His humanity, and even the Son of God trembled beneath its weight. Yet in that crushing, He began - *"Nevertheless, not My will but Yours be done."*

Gethsemane means "oil press." It is the place where what is hidden is crushed so that what is pure can flow. Before the cross was carried, surrender was chosen. Before resurrection dawned, submission was whispered.

He endured the cross *"for the joy set before Him"* (Hebrews 12:2). That joy was you.

Every overcomer must pray a Gethsemane prayer. Every beginning costs surrender. Before God brings life through you, He must first bring death to what rules you. The oil of anointing always flows from a surrendered will.

Feelings are not the enemy. They are the instruments that remind us we're still human, still reachable, still capable of compassion. Jesus Himself "was touched with the feeling of our infirmities" (Hebrews 4:15). He didn't suppress emotion - He sanctified it. The tears of Gethsemane were not weakness; they were witness. Even in anguish, He showed us that faith doesn't erase feeling - it redeems it. So when your heart aches, don't despise it. Let it remind you that your Savior understands. Let it drive you closer, not deeper into despair. Feelings are not the fuel of faith, but they are often the fragrance of it.

The Echo

From chains to gardens, the story has always been the same. Chains break when love enters. Gardens bloom when faith begins. The orphan finds a home. The barren ground finds rain. Every surrender, every step, every seed tilts the atmosphere a little closer to Heaven's design.

Faith is the seed. Family is the soil. Freedom is the harvest. And adoption is the garden where sons and daughters learn to reign.

You were never meant to survive this world's system. You were born to terraform it - to plant Heaven's culture in broken ground until every field sings again.

The same Spirit who began this work will finish it (Philippians 1:6). Creation still leans forward, waiting for the sons and daughters of God to rise (Romans 8:19).

Until then - keep beginning. Keep sowing. Keep believing. Because every echo of obedience still shapes the sound of eternity.

Faith Over Feelings

Faith does not erase emotion; it redeems it. It does not silence the storm; it anchors the soul within it.

Elijah sat beneath the broom tree and whispered, *"It is enough."* (1 Kings 19:4) Jesus knelt beneath the olive trees and cried, *"Nevertheless, not My will but Yours be done."* (Luke 22:42) Both faced the weight of exhaustion, yet both found grace waiting in the

142

shadows. The whisper that revived Elijah still speaks. The same Spirit that strengthened Jesus still breathes through you.

Faith begins when feelings end. It's the quiet decision to take one more step when your soul wants to sleep. It's lifting your eyes when despair demands you bow. It's believing that bread will come again, strength will return, and dawn will follow even the longest night.

Paul wrote, *"We live by faith, not by sight."* (2 Corinthians 5:7) And again, *"The righteous shall live by faith."* (Romans 1:17) Faith is not blindness; it is divine perspective - seeing with Heaven's eyes when the world goes dim.

When Peter sank beneath the waves, the hand of Jesus reached for him *immediately* (Matthew 14:31). That same immediacy of grace still reaches for you - not after you rise, but while you fall. Every falter is another opportunity for rescue. Every weakness is another place for strength to prove itself perfect (2 Corinthians 12:9).

And when the heart accuses - when guilt whispers, *"You'll never change"* - Scripture answers, *"God is greater than our heart, and He knows everything."* (1 John 3:20) He knows your fear, your fatigue, your faltering - and still calls you *His*.

So begin again. Plant the seed. Pray the prayer. Serve someone who feels orphaned in faith. Because Heaven does not honor perfection; it honors perseverance. Faith is not the absence of feeling - it is choosing obedience in its presence.

The righteous fall seven times and rise again (Proverbs 24:16). So rise. Whisper under your own broom tree if you must. Let the hand of Jesus lift you from the water. Let His Spirit breathe through your trembling lungs until your heart steadies again.

Today, choose to begin. Today, choose to believe. Today, choose to overcome.

You are not ruled by what you feel; you are led by who He is.

Scripture Index

#FaithOverFeelings

#SpiritBorn

#Unchained

Apostolic Equipping:

Practicing Adoption

"You shall not leave them as orphans" (John 14:18). Adoption is not an event - it's a rhythm of family. Faith grows best in relationship, where love becomes the atmosphere and belonging becomes the soil.

New believers rarely need a lecture; they need a table, a text, a touchpoint. Apostolic communities embody the Father's heart by walking with sons and daughters until they know they are home.

Kingdom Practices:
- Commit to one new believer for the next 90 days - pray daily, check in weekly (Galatians 4:5-7).
- Share one meal a week; belonging is built over bread (Acts 2:42-47).
- Read a short passage together three days a week; let the Word do the forming.
- Invite them into a small "I Am Circle" for identity declarations and mutual encouragement.
- Celebrate small victories - each day of faith is sacred ground (1 Thessalonians 2:7-12).

Adoption is not a metaphor. It's a table, a rhythm, and a relationship that reveals the Father. (James 1:27) - *"Pure religion is to care for orphans and widows in their distress."*

Chapter Thirteen

You Are a Winner

You may not feel like it. You may look at your life and see more scars than medals, more failures than trophies, more empty nights than cheering crowds. But hear me clearly: **You are a winner. Period.**

Not because you've outrun everyone else. Not because you've never stumbled. Not because your feelings agree.

You are a winner because the outcome was settled at the Cross. Jesus didn't just die *for* you - He triumphed *as* you. Every nail that pierced Him disarmed what accused you (Colossians 2:14-15). Your victory isn't pending; it's inherited.

Paul declared, *"Thanks be to God, who always leads us in triumph in Christ"* (2 Corinthians 2:14). Not sometimes. Not occasionally. Always.

Even when you limp, you're led.

Even when you weep, you're winning.

Even when you fall, grace still calls it forward motion.

You are not racing for victory - you're running from it. The Cross was the finish line. Everything since has just been the victory lap.

The Odds Were Against You

If Heaven's courts had calculated odds the way casinos do, no one would have bet on you. The weight of sin stacked against you. The record of shame nailed above you. The chains of failure rattling at your feet. Every statistic said, *"You'll fall again."* Every voice said, *"You'll never change."*

No sane gambler would have placed a wager. But God did something outrageous. He staked His Son - not as a gamble, but as a guarantee. Jesus wasn't Heaven's risk; He was Heaven's certainty. The Cross wasn't the roll of dice - it was the signing of a contract written in blood.

When the stone rolled away, Heaven cashed in the victory slip: *Paid. Won. Finished.* (John 19:30). The resurrection wasn't luck - it was law.

"Thanks be to God, who gives us the victory through our Lord Jesus Christ." (1 Corinthians 15:57). You weren't the safest bet - you were the surest redemption. Grace didn't hedge its wager; it bought you outright.

Jericho's Secret: Thanksgiving Before the Fall

Israel marched in circles around Jericho for seven days. Every lap looked the same. The dust rose. The sun burned. The walls mocked their obedience. But victory wasn't delayed - it was declared in advance: *"See, I have delivered Jericho into your hands."* (Joshua 6:2).

They weren't walking *toward* victory; they were walking it *out*. Each step was a sermon. Each lap was a declaration: *"We trust You even when nothing moves."*

How did they walk? With thanksgiving in their mouths. How did they shout? With praise already burning in their lungs.

Jehoshaphat discovered the same secret generations later. When Judah faced armies too vast to number, God told him not to send soldiers first - but singers. *"Appoint those who should sing to the Lord and who should praise the beauty of holiness."* And when they began to sing, *"the Lord set ambushes against the enemy."* (2 Chronicles 20:21-22). Praise broke what power could not. God didn't need their strength - He needed their sound.

I learned that same lesson in a country church years ago. When my wife and I began a daughter work, the church we attended didn't bless the effort. We were told not to tell anyone. We were accused of stealing because we used our own tithe to support the plant. We became outcasts - alone, misunderstood, yet certain of the call.

But there was a small building with a piano, an organ, and a guitar. So I went there and worshiped. For hours, it was just me and the Lord. No crowds. No applause. Just Presence.

Before the first soul ever walked through the door, before the first baptism, before the first shout of victory - there was worship. Not for recognition. Not for reassurance. Just for relationship. I didn't know the battles that would come, but I

148

knew this: if His Presence remained, every wall would eventually fall. If I lost that Presence, the battle would already be lost.

Moses understood that same desperation when he stood before God and said, *"If Your Presence does not go with us, do not send us up from here."* (Exodus 33:15). He refused to move without divine companionship. What good is a promised land if God isn't in it? What good is ministry without Presence? That's the posture of every true overcomer - not ambition, but dependence. We move, not because the way is clear, but because His nearness is certain.

That's the secret. Worship is not preparation for victory; it *is* victory. Praise is not noise - it's navigation. When gratitude fills the silence, Heaven fills the space. Walls crumble where worship rises. So lift your voice before the breakthrough. Because when praise precedes progress, victory becomes inevitable.

Henri Nouwen once wrote, *"The spiritual life is a life in which we wait, actively present to the moment, trusting that victory has already been won, though not yet fully seen."* (Nouwen, 1981a) [66] Faith learns to praise before proof and to rest before reward. That's what it means to march in circles with certainty.

A Story of Opposition

I remember a season when rumors spread about me - words I never said, actions I never did. People I thought were for

---

[66] Henri J.M. Nouwen, *Making All Things New* (San Francisco: HarperOne, 1981)

me turned cold. Invitations dried up. A friend stopped answering calls. The sting wasn't just the slander; it was the silence of those who believed it.

I prayed, *"God, if this is leadership, I don't want it."* But in the middle of that rejection, the Spirit whispered, *"If they walked away from Me, they will walk away from you. But their absence cannot cancel My anointing."*

One day, an older minister took me aside. He didn't offer sympathy; he offered strategy. He said, *"Don't answer your accusers. Don't chase every rumor. Keep walking, keep preaching, keep loving. If you stay faithful, time will testify. Truth will outlast the noise."*

That counsel became a compass. I stopped defending myself and started depending on God to defend His work. And He did. Slowly, quietly, the lies lost oxygen. The very mouths that spoke against me forgot their own accusations. But the fruit of faithfulness remained.

It hurt - some days it still does - but I learned this: opposition doesn't define you; obedience does. Betrayal doesn't disqualify; it refines. The voices that walk away will fade, but the voice that called you will never fall silent. If you refuse to bow to bitterness, God will make vindication your shadow.

So don't waste energy answering what God intends to outlast. Keep building. Keep believing. Because every rumor eventually runs out of breath - but the truth endures forever (Psalm 37:5-6; 1 Peter 2:23).

A Personal Defeat That Wasn't

I remember a season when I measured myself against empty pews and felt like I was losing every week. The sermons were faithful, but the seats were vacant. I watched the offering plates pass with more air than bills and wondered if obedience had become a fool's errand. One night, I cried at the altar, whispering to God that I didn't have it in me anymore.

But the Spirit whispered back, *"This isn't about attendance. This is about obedience. And obedience never loses."*

A.W. Tozer once said, *"The man or woman who belongs to Christ wins no matter how the world counts loss."* (Tozer, 1955) [67]

That night nothing changed on the outside - the crowd didn't grow, the numbers didn't shift - but something changed within me. I realized I wasn't losing. I was learning. I wasn't defeated. I was already seated in victory (Ephesians 2:6).

Peter knew that feeling. He had fished all night and caught nothing (Luke 5:5). The nets were empty, the work exhausting, the reward invisible. But when Jesus said, *"Launch out into the deep,"* Peter obeyed again - and the same water that once mocked his effort became the stage for a miracle. The catch didn't validate his skill; it vindicated his obedience.

That's the secret of Kingdom success: **fruit is never the proof of faithfulness - Presence is.** God measures victories by

---

[67] A.W. Tozer, *The Root of the Righteous* (Chicago: Moody Publishers, 1955)

alignment, not applause. As Kevin Rice wrote in *Cultivating the New Nature:* *"We must take ownership of our new nature and grow into the fullness of Christ. Victory is in the DNA, but maturity is in the process."* (Rice, 2023a) [68] As Oswald Chambers once wrote, *"God does not call us to be successful, but to be faithful."* (Chambers, 1935) [69] Faithfulness will always feel like losing before it looks like winning.

So keep casting the net. Keep preaching to the empty room. Because what feels like defeat may be the deep where miracles are about to surface. In the Kingdom, obedience is the scoreboard, and victory was already decided at the cross (1 Corinthians 15:57).

The Chains of Comparison

Comparison is a cruel chain. It doesn't just bind individuals -it fractures the Body. It whispers, *"You're behind. You're less. You don't measure up."* And while you chase someone else's pace, you abandon your own race.

Paul called this spirit by name: *emulations* - ζῆλος (*zēlos*) - the fleshly impulse to imitate another's grace instead of cultivating your own (Galatians 5:20). It is the counterfeit of calling. It looks like zeal, but it runs on envy. It performs, but it doesn't carry Presence.

---

[68] Kevin Rice, *Cultivating the New Nature* (EKI Publishing, 2021)
[69] Oswald Chambers, *My Utmost for His Highest* (Grand Rapids, MI: Discovery House Publishers, 1935)

As Galatians 5 states : *19 Now the works of the flesh are manifest, which are these; Adultery, fornication, uncleanness, lasciviousness, 20 Idolatry, witchcraft, hatred, variance, emulations, wrath, strife, seditions, heresies, 21 Envyings, murders, drunkenness, revellings, and such like: of the which I tell you before, as I have also told you in time past, that they which do such things shall not inherit the kingdom of God.*

In modern language, emulation is like running a **Windows emulation on a Mac.** It might look compatible, but it's never native - it imitates what it cannot host. That's what happens when believers try to duplicate another person's anointing: they run the wrong operating system. It works for a moment, but it crashes under the weight of authenticity.

I know this because I lived it. When I first began to preach, I was timid - nervous every time I stood behind a pulpit. I watched other ministers online, studied their cadence, copied their inflections. I thought if I could sound like them, maybe I would carry what they carried.

One night, I preached a message I had once heard another preacher deliver. Halfway through, I realized something was missing. The words were right, but the wind was gone. The message was still truth - but it wasn't *mine*. Then, in the middle of that sermon, I shifted. I stopped performing and started flowing. I leaned into my own anointing instead of trying to wear someone else's voice. And in that moment, I felt the shift. The atmosphere changed. People began to respond to the word, not with clapping but with faith and belief. Presence filled the room again.

It wasn't the message that carried power - it was the anointing that made it *mine*. (The Word is eternal, but the delivery is incarnational - He speaks through identity, not performance, through being, not pretending.)

I've watched young ministers fall into the same trap - preaching word for word what they've heard online, copying someone else's delivery down to their gestures. And like Saul's armor on David, it never fits. It might look impressive, but it restricts movement. It muffles authenticity.

It took that young minister years to find his own voice, and when he finally did, the anointing came alive. God doesn't anoint duplicates; He anoints originals.

That's why Jesus told Peter, when he asked about John's calling, *"If I will that he remain till I come, what is that to you? You follow Me."* (John 21:22). In other words, *"Run your race, Peter. Stop comparing assignments."*

Comparison is the birthplace of emulation, and emulation is the graveyard of authenticity. It is sin disguised as ambition - envy veiled in religious language.

Faith rejoices when others rise because it knows there's more than enough glory to go around. You are not racing your neighbor; you are running in Christ. He already broke the tape at the finish line (Hebrews 12:1-2).

So wear your own armor. Preach your own message. Run your own race. Because the anointing that rests on you was never designed to sound like anyone else's.

The Church doesn't need clones - it needs carriers. And Heaven is still looking for those bold enough to say, *"I will not emulate - I will embody."*

You Are A Winner

Heaven's scoreboard was settled long before your first breath. The Cross wasn't a gamble - it was a guarantee. You are not fighting *for* victory; you are fighting *from* it. You are not chasing favor; you are moving from it. The battle may still roar, but the verdict is already written: *"It is finished."* (John 19:30)

Paul wrote, *"Thanks be to God, who always leads us in triumph in Christ."* (2 Corinthians 2:14) Always - not sometimes. Not when feelings agree. Always. Even when tears blur the path, the triumph remains. Even when the odds seem stacked, grace tips the scale.

Israel circled Jericho's walls for seven days. Every lap looked the same. Dust rose, sweat dripped, but heaven's promise still stood: *"See, I have delivered Jericho into your hands."* (Joshua 6:2) Victory wasn't waiting on the final shout - it was present in every step. They didn't walk *toward* victory; they walked *out* victory.

The same is true for you. When your worship feels weary, your faith is working. When your gratitude sounds quiet, your obedience still shakes walls. Heaven doesn't grade your volume; it hears your trust.

Jehoshaphat sent singers ahead of the soldiers, and *"when they began to sing and praise, the Lord set ambushes against their enemies."* (2 Chronicles 20:22) That's heaven's paradox - worship is warfare. Praise precedes progress. Thanksgiving breaks what strength cannot.

So lift up your head, beloved. (Psalm 24:7) The odds were against you, but the Cross counted you in. Like Elisha's servant, you may only see the armies against you - but if heaven opened your eyes, you'd find the hills already ablaze with chariots of fire (2 Kings 6:17). The armies of God have not left you outnumbered; they've surrounded your struggle with strength. The enemy sneered, but grace smiled first. You were written into victory before you ever entered the fight. You are more than a conqueror through Him who loved you (Romans 8:37).

The walls are trembling. The chains are cracking. Every step of faith is another shout of triumph echoing through eternity. So give thanks before you see the answer. Shout before the walls fall. Worship while the dust still hangs in the air.

You are not the underdog; you are the inheritor. You are not running for a crown; you are wearing one. (2 Timothy 4:8) Your scars are not your shame - they are your medals. Every bruise, every battle, every breath you've given in faith has not been wasted.

The scoreboard of heaven reads one word: **Victory.** The sound of your steps is the march of the redeemed. The banner above you is love. (Song of Solomon 2:4)

You are Spirit-born. You are unchained. You are a winner - not by performance, but by possession. Not by striving, but by sonship.

And when you cross the finish line, you'll discover what faith already knew: The race was won before it began.

Scripture Index

#AlwaysTriumph

#FaithWins

#Unchained

Apostolic Equipping:

Walking Others Through Forgiveness

Opposition will come - but forgiveness keeps it from taking root. Apostolic leaders don't just endure betrayal; they redeem it. Forgiveness is not weakness - it's warfare that dismantles bitterness before it hardens.

When trust fractures, don't rush the repair. Name the wound with honesty. Invite confession where it's safe to speak. Restore gently, not reactively (Galatians 6:1).

Forgiveness doesn't erase the scar; it transforms it into testimony. Your healed places become maps for others still bleeding. This is how the Church grows whole - one restoration at a time.

Kingdom Practices:
- Pray by name for those who have wounded you.
- Share your restoration story to model reconciliation.
- Walk beside someone else learning to forgive.
- Celebrate repentance as Heaven does - with joy, not judgment.

(Ephesians 4:32) - *"Be kind and compassionate to one another, forgiving each other, just as in Christ God forgave you."*

Chapter Fourteen

Avoid Pointless Progress

The world is noisy. Screens glow. Headlines scroll. Sports scores update by the minute. Notifications buzz in our pockets like restless insects.

There is always something asking for our eyes, our ears, our time. We move endlessly. We run. We hustle. We "multi-task." And yet - how little of it matters.

Like a treadmill that keeps our legs pumping but never changes the scenery, we exhaust ourselves with motion but achieve no movement. Distraction is the new chain. Not iron. Not steel. But digital, mental, cultural. And many of us wear it without even realizing we are bound.

Distraction doesn't just steal time - it fractures presence. It isolates hearts that were meant to intertwine. We scroll through the lives of others while neglecting the ones sitting across from us. We "connect" online but forget how to truly belong.

The enemy doesn't need to chain your hands if he can capture your attention. Because what holds your attention will eventually hold your affection.

But the Spirit is calling a generation of outcasts and overcomers to live differently - to be *keepers of Presence* in a culture addicted to noise. The world doesn't need louder voices; it needs deeper ones. Voices that listen before they speak. Hearts that notice the treasure hidden in others and call it to the surface.

Every conversation can be a ministry. Every table can be a sanctuary. Every outcast you embrace is a culture shift in motion.

You change the atmosphere not by overpowering noise but by carrying peace into it. When you turn your attention to someone overlooked, Heaven leans in with you. The Kingdom advances one act of undistracted love at a time.

This is how culture turns - when Presence becomes more powerful than performance, when compassion becomes more contagious than outrage, when attention becomes intercession.

The Illusion of Progress

The world tells us progress is measured in numbers. How many points did your team score? How many likes did your post get? How many hours did you work this week? How many followers, paychecks, or promotions prove that your life is moving forward?

But Heaven doesn't track sports statistics. Heaven doesn't record your screen time as triumph. Heaven is not impressed by ladders climbed if they are leaning against the wrong wall.

We live in a culture obsessed with counting everything except what counts. We count followers but not faithfulness. We count clicks but not compassion. We count revenue but not redemption.

C.S. Lewis once observed that when *"second things"* are treated like *"first things,"* they aren't elevated - they're corrupted. (Lewis, 1970) [70] That's what misplaced loves do. They distort true progress. We run hard, but toward shadows. We win races that lead nowhere. We exhaust our souls chasing applause from platforms that will never remember our names.

Jesus asked, *"What does it profit a man to gain the whole world, yet forfeit his soul?"* (Mark 8:36). He was reminding us that some victories are just defeats with good marketing. All progress is not good progress. Some of it is just pointless motion dressed up as victory.

Heaven defines progress differently. Progress is not measured by what you build, but by what you become - maturing until you measure up to the full stature of Christ (Ephesians 4:13). It's not in the height of your platform, but the depth of your surrender. True growth looks less like climbing and more like rooting - less like achievement and more like alignment.

Some of the greatest Kingdom builders never trended. Some of the most effective ministers never filled stadiums. But they changed rooms when they walked in. They cultivated peace instead of applause. They called out treasure in others instead of competing for attention. That's Heaven's metric - transformation, not traction.

---

[70] C.S. Lewis, *God in the Dock: Essays on Theology and Ethics* (Grand Rapids: Eerdmans, 1970), essay "First and Second Things."

So slow down. Check which wall your ladder leans on. Because not every ascent is advancement. And not every winner is winning where it matters.

Mary, Martha, and the Choice of Focus

Martha worked herself into exhaustion serving Jesus. Her hands were flour-dusted, her voice sharp, her spirit restless. Every dish was an offering. Every step a sacrifice. But as she moved faster, peace moved farther.

Mary sat at His feet (Luke 10:38-42). The same Jesus was in both rooms - one was distracted by duty, the other was drawn by devotion. Martha was busy *for* Jesus. Mary was present *with* Jesus.

And Jesus said: *"Mary has chosen what is better, and it will not be taken away from her."*

Henri Nouwen once asked, *"The real question is not how much we have accomplished but whether what we have done is connected to the Kingdom of God."* (Nouwen, 1981a) [71] That is the difference between Martha and Mary: one measured her worth in what she produced; the other in whom she beheld.

The world crowns Marthas. Heaven crowns Marys. The world measures effort; Heaven measures intimacy. The world asks, *"How much did you do?"* Heaven asks, *"How much of Me did you know?"*

---

[71] Henri J.M. Nouwen, *Making All Things New* (San Francisco: HarperOne, 1981).

Martha's meal fed bodies for a moment; Mary's posture moved Heaven for eternity. Martha's labor was good, but Mary's focus was holy. Martha's striving reflected a system that says, *"Earn your place."* Mary's stillness reflected a Kingdom that whispers, *"You already belong."*

There's nothing wrong with serving - Jesus never rebuked Martha for making the meal. He simply invited her to remember why she was serving. When doing replaces dwelling, ministry becomes machinery. The same hands that build altars can also build idols if Presence isn't the focus.

We live in a culture of Marthas - always producing, always proving, always performing. But Heaven is raising a generation of Marys - those who choose the better part, those who know that *rest is not laziness but alignment.* Those who understand that *intimacy is the birthplace of impact.*

Which are you becoming? The anxious host or the adoring friend? The one who works for Jesus or the one who walks with Him? The crowd will always reward productivity. But the Kingdom will always honor presence.

Today Is a Gift

Today is called *the present* because it is a gift from God. Moses prayed, *"Teach us to number our days, that we may gain a heart of wisdom."* (Psalm 90:12). Time is not a wage you earn; it is a treasure you steward. You cannot hoard it. You cannot extend it. You can only spend it. And where you spend it reveals your heart. Jesus said, *"Where your treasure is, there your heart will be also." (Matthew 6:21).*

Kevin Rice wrote in *The Noah Generation: "Sons of God terraform culture, but they do not waste seed on barren ground. Focus is faith in action."* (Rice, 2023b)[72] Every hour is seed. Where you plant it determines whether your field is barren or fruitful.

I think often of my grandparents - now home with the Lord. Some of my richest memories were not built in grand moments, but in quiet ones. Cooking together in a kitchen filled with laughter. Working on crafts at the table. Listening to stories of God's faithfulness told in the gentle cadence of their voices. At the time, it just felt like family. Now I realize - it was formation.

They were sowing eternity into me without even knowing it. Those conversations, those shared smiles, those whispered prayers before meals - each became a deposit in the treasury of my soul. They didn't just tell me about God; they *showed* me what He looked like. Their stories of His goodness became the scaffolding of my faith. Every minute spent with them was a seed of legacy planted in my heart, one that still bears fruit long after they've gone to their eternal reward.

Time is not measured in minutes but in meaning. The present moment - when given fully - is how we participate in eternity. The people around you are not interruptions; they are investments. Your presence with them is a ministry.

---

[72] Kevin Rice, *The Noah Generation* (EKI Publishing, 2023).

We live in a world that prizes efficiency over empathy, productivity over presence. But Heaven measures differently. It's not how much you accomplished today, but how much love you invested. The stories you tell, the laughter you share, the prayers you whisper - they are the currency of Heaven.

So slow down. Look someone in the eye. Listen like their words are holy. Love like your minutes are sacred.

Today is not just another block on a calendar. It is seed in your hand and eternity in your reach. Spend it well.

Author Annie Dillard once wrote, *"How we spend our days is, of course, how we spend our lives."* (Dillard, 1989) [73] Every moment becomes the mosaic of eternity. And yet, even those who love God deeply can forget how sacred the simple moments are. Sometimes, we don't realize how precious the present is until we've run past it - until we look up from the work of ministry and realize we've left the garden of our own homes untended.

My Own Chains of Busyness

I once lived this truth the hard way. At one point, I was pastoring our main church, overseeing a daughter work eighteen miles away, and helping another church forty-five minutes down the road with their music. That church had a daughter work as well, and I was filling in wherever gaps appeared.

---

[73] Annie Dillard, *The Writing Life* (New York: Harper & Row, 1989)

In a single week, I was preaching at least three services, leading worship in seven, and spending my remaining hours on outreach. When I wasn't in ministry, I was working a secular job to support my family.

Our first son was only three years old. Our second son had just died at birth. And I was never home.

I told myself I was working for the Lord, and that He would take care of everything. But the truth was sobering: I was chained - not by sin, but by ministry itself. Chained by the expectations of others. Chained by the lie that God wanted my activity more than my presence, more than my family, more than my heart.

I was so tired I could hardly think. Finally, I had to step away from much of what I was doing to focus on the things the Lord had actually placed in my care. I learned the hard way that we can lose sight of both Him and our families while running after things we believe are "for Him."

Ministry can become a treadmill too. A holy-looking treadmill. And if we are not careful, we mistake the sweat for fruit, the noise for impact, the motion for meaning.

Chains of Distraction

Not all chains clang. Some glow on screens. Some vibrate in your pocket. Some whisper, *"Just one more scroll, one more meeting, one more song."*

The enemy doesn't need you to be wicked if he can keep you distracted. He doesn't need you rebellious if he can keep you exhausted.

A.W. Tozer once warned, *"The things that matter most must never be at the mercy of the things that matter least."* (Tozer, 1960) [74] Yet how many of us give our best hours to what matters least and our scraps to what matters most?

Distraction is not simply about technology; it's about attention. It's the subtle seduction of divided affection - the theft of focus that empties our devotion. We live in an attention economy where the loudest voices profit from our silence, and our soul pays the price.

The enemy doesn't always show up as temptation; sometimes he just shows up as noise. He knows if he can't make you sin, he'll make you scroll. If he can't make you rebel, he'll make you rush. And soon your heart will confuse stimulation with significance.

You can be unchained from shame but still shackled by busyness. You can walk out of Egypt and still wander in circles. Because distraction keeps the body moving while the heart stands still.

But God never called His sons and daughters to live fragmented. To be Spirit-born is to be free from both sin and distraction - free to be fully present with Him, and therefore fully

---

[74] A.W. Tozer, *Of God and Men* (Chicago: Moody Publishers, 1960).

alive in the world. Presence breaks the cycle. Stillness becomes warfare. Focus becomes intercession.

In a noisy world, attention is worship. When you fix your gaze on Jesus, you reclaim what culture has stolen - your wonder, your peace, your awareness of the holy moments right in front of you.

And here's the secret: the more present you are with Him, the more prophetic you become to others. Because every focused heart becomes a living invitation for others to see clearly again.

So put down what drains you. Silence what divides you. And return your eyes to the One who never competes for your attention - He simply waits for it.

Paul's Race

Paul wrote, *"Do you not know that in a race all the runners run, but only one gets the prize? Run in such a way as to get the prize."* (1 Corinthians 9:24).

It is possible to run hard and still lose if you're running in the wrong direction. It is possible to exhaust yourself chasing shadows but never touch the crown. Paul refused pointless progress. He ran with focus. He aimed his steps. He lived not for the applause of men but for the prize of Christ.

When I was a kid, I didn't grow up playing sports seriously. Most of what I learned came from the church gym, where the older kids dominated one end of the court while the rest of us made do with the other. We played half-court so often that it became our entire frame of reference.

One night, the older group left early, and we finally had the full court to ourselves. During one play, I grabbed a rebound, dribbled out to midcourt, turned around, and drove straight back toward the hoop I'd always aimed for. I made the shot - clean, perfect, right through the net. I was shocked I'd hit it... until I realized it was the wrong basket.

Everyone laughed, but I remember the feeling sinking deep into my chest. I'd run hard, aimed confidently, even celebrated the score - but I was running the wrong way the whole time.

Years later, I understood that moment was a parable. Effort means nothing if it's aimed in the wrong direction. You can sweat in the gym of life, pour yourself into ministry, work, or even good causes, and still be scoring points for the wrong team. Paul's race wasn't about activity - it was about alignment. He ran toward the upward call, not sideways ambition. He disciplined his body, yes, but he directed his heart.

David Webb once put it this way: *"When the church trades Presence for programs, she wins crowds but loses Christ."* (Webb, 2025a) [75] That's Paul's warning in modern language: don't confuse speed for Spirit, or crowds for crowns.

---

[75] David Webb, *Building the Kingdom in the Local Church* (EKI Publishing, 2025)

There's a kind of busyness that looks like winning - schedules full, events packed, applause loud - but Heaven calls it wasted motion. Paul didn't want to be disqualified after preaching to others (1 Corinthians 9:27). He understood the danger of living efficiently in the wrong direction.

Every runner must eventually ask: *Whose finish line am I chasing?* Because in the Kingdom, success is not crossing first - it's crossing faithful. Run, yes - but run with focus. Run with your eyes fixed on Jesus. Run toward the right prize

The Shock Line

Let me make it plain, so no chain of confusion remains.

Heaven does not care who won last year's championship. Heaven is not moved by how many hours you binged your favorite series. Heaven is not impressed by your busy calendar if it is chained to the trivial. Heaven does not applaud what keeps you distracted while your destiny waits untouched.

We live like eternity is a rumor, as if tomorrow is guaranteed, as if God owes us another sunrise. But every tick of the clock is mercy - borrowed breath from the One who could call it back in a moment.

One day, eternity will ask: *What did you do with the hours I gave you?* Not the hours you posted, but the ones you wasted. Not the stages you stood on, but the lives you stood beside. Not the projects you started, but the people you served.

This is not guilt. This is invitation. A wake-up call. A chain snapping. The sound of grace shouting through the static: *"Wake up, sleeper, and rise from the dead, and Christ will shine on you."* (Ephesians 5:14).

Heaven's scoreboard looks nothing like Earth's. The trophies are souls, not statistics. The wins are measured in obedience, not algorithms. The reward is Presence, not platform.

You can't Netflix your way into purpose. You can't scroll your way into legacy. You can't multitask your way into anointing. God doesn't need another influencer - He's looking for an intercessor.

This is the line in the sand. The shock line. The moment you stop living entertained and start living engaged. Because when you stop chasing the meaningless, you make room for the miraculous.

So wake up. Put down the chains of comfort. Lift your eyes off the temporary. And live like time is holy again.

The Gift of Stillness

The world worships motion. Screens glow. Calendars overflow. Notifications buzz like flies on sacred moments. And yet, for all our movement, how little of it moves heaven.

We sprint through days that were meant to be walked with God. We climb ladders that lean against the wrong walls. We mistake noise for significance and exhaustion for effectiveness.

But Jesus still whispers the same invitation: *"Come to Me, all who are weary and burdened, and I will give you rest."* (Matthew 11:28)

He doesn't call the lazy; He calls the overloaded. He doesn't condemn the busy; He reorders their steps.

When Martha ran herself ragged serving, Mary sat at His feet (Luke 10:38 - 42). Martha was working *for* Jesus; Mary was resting *with* Him. And Jesus said, *"Mary has chosen what is better, and it will not be taken away from her."* (Luke 10:42)

Every chain of distraction begins with misplaced devotion. Every moment reclaimed begins with rediscovered Presence.

David prayed, *"Teach us to number our days, that we may gain a heart of wisdom."* (Psalm 90:12) He knew time was sacred currency - not to be spent on shadows, but invested in Presence. Time is not a wage you earn; it is a treasure you steward. Every breath is borrowed grace, a countdown of mercy, a rhythm of divine opportunity.

C.S. Lewis once wrote that *"The future is something which everyone reaches at the rate of sixty minutes an hour, whatever he does, whoever he is."* (Lewis, 1942) [76] But not everyone reaches it wisely. The difference between the weary and the fruitful is not speed - it's focus.

Jesus said, *"Where your treasure is, there your heart will be also."* (Matthew 6:21) Your time reveals your treasure. If your schedule

---

[76] C.S. Lewis, *The Screwtape Letters* (New York: HarperOne, 2015; originally published 1942)

cannot find space for the Savior, your pace has become your prison.

Heaven defines progress differently. It's not how much you build, but how deeply you abide (John 15:5). It's not how high you climb, but how faithfully you sit. True fruit is born, not forced. And true rest is not inactivity - it is alignment.

The Lord of eternity does not applaud motion; He rewards presence. So silence the false urgency. Step off the treadmill. Sit at His feet before you run in His name.

You are not called to hurry. You are called to holiness. You are not measured by noise, but by nearness. You are Spirit-born. You are unchained. You will not waste this gift.

Scripture Index

#FocusedFaith

#SpiritBorn

#Unchained

Apostolic Equipping:

Practicing Holy Boundaries

Boundaries are not walls - they are wisdom. They are how love remains sustainable in a world addicted to hurry. To live unchained, you must learn when to say *no* so your *yes* still carries weight.

Jesus withdrew often to pray (Luke 5:16). Even the Savior of the world honored margin. Apostolic culture guards presence over pressure. Boundaries are not selfish - they are stewardship.

Ask often: *Is this mine to carry, or is this another's burden?* (Galatians 6:5) Freedom deepens when you stop rescuing what God is refining.

Kingdom Practices:
- Create sacred pauses in your week for prayer, rest, and family.
- Say "no" to what drains you so you can say "yes" to what builds others.
- Model boundaries for others; let margin become contagious.

(Luke 5:16) - *"Jesus often withdrew to lonely places and prayed."*

Chapter Fifteen

The 7 Subtle Chains

Some chains don't shatter in fire -they wither in silence. They're not forged in rebellion but woven in routine. You don't feel them at first. You call them discipline, duty, balance, survival. But slowly, quietly, they start to wrap around the roots of your soul.

The Spirit once whispered to me, *"Not every chain makes noise."* That sentence haunted me. Because the loud ones - the sins, the scandals, the public failures - we know how to drag those to the altar. But the quiet ones? We baptize those in busyness, polish them with excuses, and wear them like badges of honor.

These are the subtle chains. They don't break your shout; they choke your growth. They don't make you quit; they make you numb. They blend into the soil of good intentions until you can't tell the difference between faithfulness and fatigue.

This is the battlefield most believers never name. The weeds that grow in the same field as your wheat. But if we're going to be truly unchained, we can't just cast out the obvious - we must confront the ordinary. So, let's drag them into the light. Not to shame ourselves, but to set ourselves free.

The enemy rarely storms through the front door with banners raised and horns blasting. He is more patient than that. He sows weeds quietly, in the night, while no one is watching.

Jesus told us: *"The kingdom of heaven is like a man who sowed good seed in his field. But while everyone was sleeping, his enemy came and sowed weeds among the wheat"* (Matthew 13:24-25).

Not all chains clang. Some lie silent, disguised as ordinary habits, wrapping around the roots of your faith until life is strangled. We look for fiery attacks, but most of the time, the enemy plants whispers. We expect bombs, but he prefers links. And sometimes he prefers vines.

In the ancient world, when iron was scarce, men twisted living vines and reeds into ropes to bind prisoners or tether animals. (Barber, 1991; Frazer, 1890) [77] [78] What grew to climb trees or shade fields could, in cunning hands, be turned into shackles. Pliny wrote of wild vines that strangled trees until they collapsed. (Elder, 1945) [79] What was meant to be life-giving became a noose.

Weeds choke growth. Chains choke breath. Both are subtle, both are deadly. Let us drag these seven subtle chains into the light before they harden around your heart.

---

[77] James George Frazer, *The Golden Bough* (London: Macmillan, 1890)
[78] Elizabeth Wayland Barber, *Prehistoric Textiles: The Development of Cloth in the Neolithic and Bronze Ages with Special Reference to the Aegean* (Princeton: Princeton University Press, 1991)
[79] Pliny the Elder, *Natural History*, trans. H. Rackham (Cambridge: Harvard University Press, Loeb Classical Library, 1945),

1. The Distracted Soldier

Paul told Timothy: *"No one serving as a soldier gets entangled in civilian affairs, but rather tries to please his commanding officer"* (2 Timothy 2:4).

But how often do we get tangled - Not by obvious rebellion, but by distraction?

The distracted soldier still wears the uniform, still salutes, still shows up for duty. But his mind is elsewhere. His weapon droops while his thumbs scroll. His loyalties slowly drift from the Commander to the chatter of the camp.

Henri Nouwen wrote that *"the greatest danger to intimacy with God is not hostility but distraction."* (Nouwen, 1981b) [80]
The enemy rarely steals your armor; he just steals your attention.

I learned this once in the middle of a prayer meeting. My mouth was praying, but my mind was building next week's sermon outline. The Spirit whispered gently: *"You're talking to Me about Me, but you're not with Me."* That day, I realized distraction is disconnection disguised as devotion.

2. The Rule-Breaking Athlete

Paul also used the image of an athlete: *"Similarly, anyone who competes as an athlete does not receive the victor's crown except by competing according to the rules"* (2 Timothy 2:5).

---

[80] Henri J.M. Nouwen, *The Way of the Heart* (New York: HarperOne, 1981)

The rule-breaking athlete trains, sweats, disciplines - and still loses - because he cuts corners in secret. But shortcuts won't catch up to you.

The chain here is *entitlement*: the quiet lie that says, *"The rules apply to everyone but me."* C.S. Lewis said, "Integrity is doing the right thing, even when no one is watching." (Lewis, 2006) [81]

I remember giving an exam one year when I taught at a university in the south. As I graded papers, I realized several students had copied entire sections from the internet. Their answers looked brilliant - eloquent, polished, impressive - but they weren't their own.

They had the right words, but not the understanding. The content was accurate, but the heart was absent.

As I stared at those papers, the Lord spoke to me: *"Borrowed words don't carry borrowed weight."*

Truth can't be plagiarized. The Spirit anoints authenticity, not imitation. You can repeat revelation, but you can't reproduce anointing without ownership.

Integrity is Heaven's steroid - it strengthens what effort alone never can.

The weeds of compromise start small - just one broken boundary, one bent truth. But soon the whole field is compromised.

---

[81] C.S. Lewis, quoted in *Collected Letters, Vol. 3* (San Francisco: HarperSanFrancisco, 2006

3. The Procrastinating Farmer

"The hardworking farmer should be the first to receive a share of the crops." (2 Timothy 2:6). But procrastination kills harvests. Not scandal. Not sin. Just delay. "I'll sow tomorrow." "I'll pray later." "I'll forgive when I feel like it."

The procrastinating farmer doesn't waste seed; he wastes seasons. And seasons, once lost, don't return.

Kevin Rice wrote in Cultivating the New Nature: "Transformation happens as we cooperate with God's timing. Delay is not neutral - it reshapes the field of the heart." (Rice, 2023a) [82]

I once postponed reconciling with a friend after a disagreement. Weeks became months. Then I heard he was gravely ill. Standing at his hospital bed, I realized the apology I'd planned for "later" had nearly become too late. The Spirit whispered, *"Forgiveness is the only seed that grows when planted immediately."*

4. The Aimless Sprinter

Paul wrote to Corinth, *"I do not run like someone running aimlessly."* (1 Corinthians 9:26). The aimless sprinter runs hard - but with no finish line. All motion. No mission. All exhaustion. No advancement.

---

[82] Kevin Rice, *Cultivating the New Nature* (EKI Publishing, 2021)

I know this chain. There was a season when I filled every square of my calendar with ministry - preaching, leading worship, outreach - believing that motion equaled impact. But I was sprinting in circles, burning energy without gaining ground. I wasn't advancing; I was orbiting. I was running around the very things I was letting die, mistaking motion for momentum, busyness for fruit.

A.W. Tozer warned, *"The things that matter most must never be at the mercy of the things that matter least."* (Tozer, 1948) [83] I learned that the hard way. Activity without assignment is just anxiety in disguise.

Paul didn't run to prove he could move; he ran because he had seen the prize. Focus gave him endurance. Vision gave him direction. Heaven doesn't reward speed - it crowns alignment.

5. The Unreliable Laborer

"It is required that those who have been given a trust must prove faithful" (1 Corinthians 4:2).

The unreliable laborer doesn't fail because of a lack of talent or gifting, but because of inconsistency. They show up sometimes. Pray sometimes. Obey sometimes. Faithfulness is not glamorous - but it is Heaven's currency.

The chain of unreliability whispers: *"Faithfulness is optional."* They are woven one strand at a time - like vines curling silently

---

[83] A.W. Tozer, *The Pursuit of God* (Chicago: Moody Press, 1948)

around a branch, until the weight of neglect bends it to the ground. What begins as a single skipped moment becomes a pattern, and what becomes a pattern becomes a chain.

But heaven doesn't reward brilliance - it rewards consistency. David Webb put it sharply: "The Kingdom advances not on giftedness but on dependability. God trusts faithful hands, not fickle ones." (Webb, 2025a) [84]

I know a man who discovered this truth the hard way. After serving thirty days in jail out west, he was released on work release and carried a heavy sense of shame. He longed to serve, but fear chained him to hesitation.

He would volunteer at church only to pull back when children were present - afraid of how people saw him, afraid of being accused, afraid of repeating the story that haunted his past. His unreliability wasn't born of laziness; it was born of fear. He wanted to be seen as valuable, but the more unreliable he became, the less people trusted him. And the less they trusted him, the less valuable he felt.

But one day, in a church service, a leader walked up to him and asked, *"Have you ever worked in audiovisual?"* He had not. Yet the leader placed headphones on his ears, showed him the basics, and gave him responsibility that mattered.

---

[84] David Webb, *Building the Kingdom in the Local Church* (EKI Publishing, 2025)

There were no children in that department, no shadows of accusation - only faithfulness required. And in that booth this man discovered that reliability could be reborn. He found a place where he could serve, be trusted, and rediscover his worth. Chains of fear began to break. Dependability was resurrected. Faithfulness healed what fear fractured.

6. The Heavy-Burdened Runner

Hebrews 12:1 tells us: *"Let us throw off everything that hinders and the sin that so easily entangles. And let us run with perseverance the race marked out for us."* Not every weight is wicked. Some are just heavy.

The heavy-burdened runner isn't always weighed down by sin. Sometimes it's just baggage: guilt, shame, people-pleasing, old regrets.

I once carried grief from a son I buried before he ever took a breath. We prayed. We fasted. We pleaded with heaven for his life. But he died at birth.

The silence of that moment was louder than any scream. And I turned the blade inward - I blamed myself. I whispered that it must have been because of some sin long ago. That my past had come to collect.

The weight of that lie bent me low, nearly breaking me in half. Until I saw it - Jesus had already carried that weight up a hill. The cross was bent beneath it so I wouldn't have to be. I didn't need to walk through life stooped in shame. I could stand upright, because He had bowed under it for me.

I didn't have to run bent over.

Henri Nouwen called this "the burden of the self-rejecting heart." (Nouwen, 1981b) [85] The chains of heaviness convince you that you must drag every failure forever. But Christ says, *"My yoke is easy, and my burden is light"* (Matthew 11:30).

7. The Shadowboxer

Paul closes the image: *"I do not fight like a boxer beating the air"* (1 Corinthians 9:26).

The shadowboxer looks busy - swings wildly, arms flailing, heart pounding, fists pumping - but strikes nothing. Motion without contact. Energy without impact. Battle without victory. Sweat without breakthrough.

Prayer without faith.

Service without love.

Activity without impact.

Tradition without meaning.

Ceremony without revelation.

I once worked beside a man who spent hours "organizing." His desk overflowed, his schedule packed - but nothing changed. He was exhausting himself fighting air. But his fruit was empty. He had motion, but no movement. Effort, but no effect.

---

[85] Henri J.M. Nouwen, *The Way of the Heart* (New York: HarperOne, 1981)

The shadowboxer's chain is wasted energy - the lie that busyness equals effectiveness. It is commotion disguised as commitment. It looks productive but leaves no bruises on the darkness. He grows tired from the fight, but never topples an enemy..

The Call to Weed the Field

Jesus said the weeds will grow until harvest, but He also gave us the power to cultivate.

These seven weeds that form chains around our spiritual growth are not dramatic sins - they are subtle. They are distractions, shortcuts, delays, weights, inconsistencies, wasted energy. And because they are subtle, they are more dangerous than we realize. They choke slowly. They whisper, *"You're fine."* They hide beneath the language of responsibility.

But here is the good news: the Spirit that raised Jesus from the dead lives in you (Romans 8:11). You don't fight weeds with willpower; you overcome them with resurrection life.

In my garden at home, I've learned something strange: weeds pull up easiest the day after rain. The soil softens; roots release. The same is true in the Spirit. When the rain of His Presence falls, chains loosen. When mercy moistens the ground of your heart, what once gripped tight begins to yield.

So invite the rain. Name the weeds. Uproot the subtle chains before they harden into iron. And watch the field of your life breathe again.

Freedom rarely begins with thunder - it begins with honesty. Chains lose their strength the moment they are named. Every weed uprooted is a space reclaimed for fruitfulness.

Don't rush this. Walk slowly through your field. Ask the Spirit to show you where you've mistaken vines for virtues, motion for maturity, noise for nearness. Let Him rain on the hardened ground until the roots release.

You are not being exposed; you are being cultivated. The Gardner never pulls weeds to humiliate the soil - He does it to make room for life. The same hands that prune are the hands that plant.

Every subtle chain broken is an echo of Eden restored. Every obedient surrender is a resurrection seed. Let Him tend what you've hidden. Let the field breathe again.

The Gift of Stillness

Stillness is not weakness. It is warfare. In a world addicted to noise, stillness is rebellion - the sacred act of returning to Presence when everything else demands performance.

C.S. Lewis once imagined hell's most effective tactic was not corruption, but distraction. *"You will find that anything or nothing is sufficient to attract his wandering attention,"* the tempter brags in *The*

185

Screwtape Letters, "until he wastes his life in the trivial." (Lewis, 1942) [86] Hell doesn't need to make you sinful if it can make you busy. It doesn't need to chain your hands if it can keep your mind racing.

But heaven's rhythm moves at a slower pace. The Kingdom does not sprint - it sows. The Spirit is not frantic - He flows.

Elijah learned this after the fire and the earthquake, when God's voice came not in the noise, but in a whisper (1 Kings 19:11 - 12). Stillness didn't mean God was absent; it meant God was near. That whisper was heaven's breath breaking through the static.

David understood it too when he wrote, *"Be still, and know that I am God."* (Psalm 46:10) To "be still" is not passive - it is prophetic. It means surrendering control, silencing hurry, and remembering Who sits on the throne.

C.S. Lewis also warned that hell's "business is to get [humans] away from the eternal and from the Present." (Lewis, 1942) [87] That is why the Spirit keeps calling us back to this moment - not yesterday's regret or tomorrow's anxiety, but now. Because *now* is where eternity touches time. Stillness is the meeting point of heaven and earth.

---

[86] C.S. Lewis, *The Screwtape Letters* (New York: HarperOne, 2015 [orig. pub. 1942]), Letter XII.
[87] Ibid., Letter XV.

When you learn to be still, you begin to see differently. The trivial loses its pull. The urgent bows to the eternal. The noise that once ruled you fades into holy silence.

The world will call that wasted time. But heaven calls it worship.

Fruit That Remains

Not all chains clang. Some whisper. Some grow like vines, slow and silent, until they wrap around the roots of purpose.

Jesus warned, *"The cares of this world and the deceitfulness of riches choke the word, and it becomes unfruitful."* (Mark 4:19) The enemy rarely storms the gate shouting; he plants weeds in the dark. (Matthew 13:25) He doesn't always tempt you to sin - sometimes he just keeps you busy.

The seven subtle chains - distraction, compromise, delay, aimlessness, inconsistency, heaviness, and fruitless activity - are not loud sins, but quiet assassins. They drain strength, dull hunger, and disguise captivity as productivity.

But the same Spirit who raised Jesus from the dead lives in you (Romans 8:11). And where the Spirit of the Lord is, there is freedom (2 Corinthians 3:17).

The soldier who once fought aimlessly can refocus. The athlete who bent the rules can return to integrity. The farmer who delayed sowing can still plant before the season ends. The weary laborer can rise and work again. Because grace does not just forgive the past - it reclaims the harvest.

Jesus said, *"Every branch in Me that bears fruit He prunes, that it may bear more fruit."* (John 15:2) Pruning feels like loss, but it's actually preparation. The Gardener cuts only what threatens the vine's future. And what feels like subtraction becomes multiplication in His hands.

You were not born to maintain barren soil. You were planted for fruit that remains (John 15:16). You were not redeemed to run in circles, but to run with endurance (Hebrews 12:1). You were not called to shadowbox the air, but to strike true in prayer and purpose (1 Corinthians 9:26).

So let the Spirit pull up the weeds. Let Him burn what no longer belongs. Let Him replace motion with mission, and habit with holiness.

The chains of distraction fall when focus returns to the Father. The weeds of compromise die when the soil drinks grace again. And the barren field blooms when the sower remembers why he began.

Lift your eyes, soldier. The harvest is still ahead. (John 4:35) Your field is not forsaken. Your seed is not wasted. Your roots are still alive.

You are Spirit-born. You are unchained. You are fruitful. Not by striving, but by abiding. Not by noise, but by nearness. Not by willpower, but by the wind of the Spirit.

Abide, and the weeds will wither. Run, and the weights will fall. Sow, and the harvest will come.

Because in the Kingdom, even the broken ground still grows.

Scripture Index

#SpiritBorn

#Unchained

#FruitThatRemains

Apostolic Equipping:

Discerning Subtle Chains

Not every chain clatters. Some hum quietly beneath routine - habits that feel harmless until they harden. Apostolic discernment means learning to notice them early, before they tighten.

Freedom begins with recognition. Ask gentle questions that surface what hides:

What is draining your joy?

What competes for your attention?

Then listen - not for excuses, but for the faint sound of links forming.

Discernment is never suspicion; it is love with ears. We name chains not to shame, but to guide. When one link breaks, another often follows. Stay close until they all fall away.

Kingdom Practices:
- Pray daily for eyes to recognize subtle bondage in yourself and others.
- Ask Spirit-led questions that expose distraction and delay.
- Celebrate small breaks in the chain as full victories in progress.
- Gather with trusted believers weekly to share what the Spirit reveals - make discernment a rhythm of community, not isolation.

(Galatians 6:1-2) - *"Restore such a one in a spirit of gentleness... and bear one another's burdens."*

Chapter Sixteen

If You Are Not Winning, It's Not Over

What do you do when you've prayed until your throat aches, fought until your fists are raw, endured until your soul feels like smoke - and still it feels like the chains are winning?

What do you do when you've dropped the chains at the altar, only to wake up with them clanging at your ankles again? When people keep fastening broken shackles back on you with their words? When you catch yourself picking them up with your own hands, ashamed and angry at the cycle?

I've been there. I've stood in the dim light of my own disappointment, whispering, "God, why am I still here? Why does freedom feel temporary? Why does victory feel like vapor?" And in the stillness, I felt Him whisper back, *"You are still standing. And standing is winning."*

Here is the truth that will not bend: If you are not winning, it is not over. The cross has the final word. The grave has the final shout. The chains are already broken. The prison door is standing open. What remains is learning to live as though it is true.

Freedom isn't a feeling - it's a fact sealed in blood. Your emotions may echo defeat, but Heaven has already recorded your victory. The struggle is not evidence of failure; it's proof that your faith is still alive. The war you're in is not about your weakness -

it's about your worth. The enemy doesn't fight the worthless; he fights the anointed.

So even when the battle drags, lift your head. Every round of resistance is writing testimony. Every time you refuse to quit, Hell loses ground. Every time you rise again, resurrection gets louder.

Maybe the chains are rattling not because you're still bound, but because freedom is shaking the last fragments loose. Maybe the noise you hear isn't defeat - it's deliverance in progress.

The same Spirit that raised Jesus from the dead lives in you (Romans 8:11). And resurrection doesn't know how to quit. It doesn't bow to relapse, delay, or disappointment. It keeps coming back stronger. It keeps breathing life into what you thought was finished.

So no matter what the scoreboard says, no matter how many times you've fallen, no matter how long you've waited - if you are not winning, it's not over.

The cross settled your score. The empty tomb rewrote your ending. You don't fight *for* victory anymore; you fight *from* it.

And if all you can do today is breathe faith through a cracked whisper, Heaven still calls that victory's sound.

The Chains Others Place Back

From the first page of this book, I told you: people will try to put chains back on you. They will remind you of your failures.

They will reduce you to labels you no longer wear. They will use your past as proof against your present.

And those chains can feel heavier than iron - because they don't come from strangers, but from those you trusted. Sometimes even from the voices that once prayed for your freedom. The wound doesn't sting because the words are sharp; it stings because the voices are familiar.

Some will whisper, "I remember what you did." Others will call your growth "pretense." They'll confuse your deliverance with denial, and your redemption with manipulation. They'll try to hold you accountable to a version of yourself that no longer exists.

But here's the truth: those chains are already broken. They are theater props, not shackles. They only hold power if you agree to carry them. You cannot be bound by what Heaven has already declared finished.

When the resurrected Christ showed His scars to Thomas, it wasn't to prove His pain - it was to prove His freedom. The marks remained, but the wounds were healed. That's how redemption works: your scars stay as testimony, not as evidence for your accusers.

There will always be people who prefer the sound of your chains to the sound of your worship - because your freedom exposes their fear. But you are not called to convince them; you are called to continue. You don't owe explanations to those who only come to inspect your wounds. You owe worship to the One who healed them.

So when voices from your past start clanging again, smile. Let them echo. They're just the sound of empty metal - remnants of what can't hold you anymore.

The cross already decided your verdict. You are not the sum of what you did, but the proof of what He's done. Your name is written, not erased. Your future is sealed, not suspended.

The greatest defiance you can offer to accusation is consistency. Keep walking free. Keep showing up redeemed. Keep living unashamed. Eventually, even your critics will have to reconcile with your fruit.

Freedom doesn't mean forgetting who hurt you - it means refusing to let their memory dictate your movement. You can't stop them from talking, but you can stop handing them your keys. You can't control their labels, but you can outlive them.

So walk on. Let the old verdicts rust behind you. You don't need to silence the voices when God has already silenced the sentence.

The Chains We Pick Back Up

Not every chain comes from someone else. Some we build ourselves. Some we willingly pick back up - because shame feels familiar, because busyness numbs pain, because despair whispers that we deserve no better.

Paul admitted the same war inside himself: *"I do not do the good I want to do, but the evil I do not want to do - this I keep on doing."* (Romans 7:19). Freedom had been given, yet his flesh kept reaching for the old restraints. It wasn't rebellion - it was reflex.

I know that reflex. There were seasons when silence felt too heavy, so I filled it with noise. When grace felt too light, I wrapped myself in guilt just to feel something with weight again. Sometimes the cage feels safer than the sky because at least you know its dimensions. But captivity, even familiar captivity, is still death in disguise.

We pick up chains because they give us structure when trust feels uncertain. We reach for control when surrender feels like falling. We run back to patterns that hurt us because they are predictable, and predictability masquerades as peace.

But the truth still stands: Even when you stumble back into the prison, the door is still unlocked. Christ already broke the lock. The chain is broken even if you still feel its weight in your hands. You may hold it, but it no longer holds you.

The prodigal's return didn't start at the father's house - it started in the pigpen when he remembered who he was. Freedom begins the same way: when you realize you're still wearing the ring even if you've been walking in the mud. Identity outlasts relapse.

So drop what no longer binds you. Lay down the self-made shackles of guilt, control, perfectionism, and fear. You don't need to punish yourself for what Jesus already paid for. Repentance is not re-sentencing - it's returning. And every return is met by a running Father.

You can't out-sin the cross. You can't out-fail His mercy. You can't reforge what He has already melted in grace.

So if you find a chain in your hand tonight, don't hide it. Lift it. Hold it up like a trophy of grace. Because even the evidence of your weakness is now proof of His victory.

My Story of Brokenness

I know this truth not in theory but in blood and tears.

There was a season when I nearly lost everything. I was pastoring one church, helping plant another eighteen miles away, and driving forty-five minutes to lead worship for yet another congregation and its daughter work. On top of that, I worked a secular job to keep food on the table.

I thought I was winning for the Lord. But behind the pulpit, I was crumbling.

Our first son was three years old. Our second son had just died at birth. And instead of sitting in the grief with my wife, I buried myself in ministry. I told myself I was serving God, but the truth was I was running from pain.

I left my wife to grieve alone while I busied myself with church work. Shame haunted me for years. I didn't even realize I was grieving - I was trying to out-preach, out-sing, and out-serve the silence of loss.

If God's grace had not caught me, I would have burned out, lost my family, and eventually fallen into ruin. I would have destroyed myself with despair and regret.

But His mercy stopped me. He forced me to lay down what I thought was holy but was killing me. He showed me that busyness is not fruit, and chains of ministry can strangle just as surely as chains of sin.

I did not come away unscathed. The shame of my absence remained. The guilt of not holding my wife when she needed me most stayed with me for years. But even scarred, I was not abandoned. Even wounded, I was not finished.

Grace pulled me from the brink. And grace will pull you, too.

The Whisper of Defeat

Elijah knew this despair. The same prophet who stood unflinching before kings, who called down fire from heaven, now lay curled under a broom tree whispering, *"It is enough; take my life."* (1 Kings 19:4). The man who outran Ahab's chariot now barely had the strength to crawl.

This is what the whisper of defeat sounds like. It tells you the battle erased the calling. It tells you your best days are behind you. It tells you that one collapse cancels every victory that came before.

But God did not send death - He sent bread. Not an end, but provision. Not a grave, but strength for the road (1 Kings 19:5-8). He did not rebuke Elijah for his collapse; He nourished him back to movement.

Elijah thought the game was over. Heaven said, *"Rise, the journey is not done."* He thought he was alone; God revealed a remnant of seven thousand who had never bowed to Baal (1 Kings 19:18). He thought his ministry was finished; God sent him to anoint Elisha and kings yet to come.

This is how God meets despair - not with scolding, but with sustenance. He gives bread for the journey and whisper for the soul. He restores perspective and community. He reminds you that collapse is not conclusion.

And the same voice is speaking over you now: *"Rise. Eat. The journey is not over."* If you are not winning, it is not over. Your exhaustion is not evidence of failure; it is an invitation to be fed. Your collapse is not the end of your calling; it's the place where God rewrites your next chapter.

The whisper of defeat says, *"You're finished."* The whisper of God says, *"You're not done; you're being refilled."*

So take the bread. Take the rest. Take the reminder that Heaven still has assignments with your name on them. You're not washed up; you're being filled up. Rise - the journey is not done.

The Head, Not the Tail

Moses told Israel: *"The Lord will make you the head, not the tail. You will always be at the top, never at the bottom."* (Deuteronomy 28:13). That wasn't a promise of perfection; it was a declaration of position. The head leads. The tail reacts. The head moves by direction. The tail moves by pressure.

To walk as the head is to live from divine initiative, not human reaction. It means you stop letting circumstance dictate motion and start letting calling dictate direction. Winning isn't pretending you've never stumbled - it's refusing to stop getting up. Losing one battle does not decide the war.

In the Kingdom, winning rarely looks like it does on earth. To Paul, victory looked like prison walls turning into pulpits. To Jesus, it looked like a cross that became a throne. To the disciples, it looked like persecution that spread the gospel like fire. Because in the Kingdom, **winning looks like influencing people with His Presence** - bringing light into dark rooms, peace into chaos, and love into hostile ground. Winning is not about what you have done, but about what He does through your obedience. Heaven calls it victory every time His Presence changes a heart.

David Webb put it plainly: "Overcoming is not surviving - it is advancing. God calls His people to move forward when retreat feels safest." (Webb, 2025b) [88] You can't lead if you're

---

[88] David Webb, *Escape from the Shame of Babylon* (EKI Publishing, 2025)

always looking back. Faith doesn't follow fear's tug; it sets Heaven's pace.

If you feel buried, remember - seeds are buried too. And seeds rise. A burial and a planting look identical from the outside, but one ends in death, the other in resurrection. When you're covered by the weight of circumstances, Heaven may simply be giving you soil to grow in.

Sometimes "top" and "bottom" are just two sides of the same process. Joseph was in a pit before he sat in a palace. Daniel knelt among lions before he stood before kings. Jesus lay in a tomb before He sat on the throne.

Burial is the disguise of breakthrough. Every head once bowed will rise again. Every seed that breaks open fulfills its design. Every child of God carries resurrection DNA.

So stop judging your position by your perspective. You may look low right now, but Heaven is still writing *upward*. You are not the tail being dragged by circumstance - you are the head being led by promise.

When God said, "You will be the head," He wasn't escribing achievement; He was describing alignment. Your victory is not in performance, but in position. As long as you are in Christ, you are already above, not beneath. Your story may bend, but it will never end in defeat.

So rise, even if it's slow. Lead, even if you limp. Because grace is the crown that never slips.

Leading Yourself Forward

The hardest person you will ever lead is yourself. It's easier to organize a team than to tame a thought. Easier to preach courage than to practice it when the room is empty. Easier to cast vision for others than to confront the hesitation hiding in your own heart.

Paul confessed this battle openly: *"I do not do the good I want to do, but the evil I do not want to do - this I keep on doing."* (Romans 7:19). That wasn't hypocrisy - it was humanity. Even apostles wrestled with alignment between intention and action.

Kevin Rice writes in *Cultivating the New Nature: "Our spiritual man is reborn unto God's purpose… but growth requires conscious cooperation. We must put on the new man daily."* (Rice, 2023a) [89] Grace births you; cooperation matures you. The new nature is a gift, but walking in it is a choice repeated sunrise after sunrise.

Victory is not one grand act of willpower - it is daily, intentional surrender. Each morning you choose again to drop the chains. Each morning you step into the freedom already purchased. Freedom isn't maintained by momentum but by mindfulness - remembering who you are before the world reminds you who you were.

Self-leadership means preaching the gospel to your own reflection before you preach it to anyone else. It means telling your

---

[89] Kevin Rice, *Cultivating the New Nature* (EKI Publishing, 2021)

soul what truth already knows: *You are free. You are forgiven. You are still called.*

It is letting the Spirit set the agenda for your emotions. It is deciding, before the day begins, that peace will be your default and obedience your language. It is learning to speak gently to yourself when shame tries to shout.

Because you can't lead others into freedom if you keep living like a prisoner on parole, authority over others begins with alignment within. When you learn to shepherd your own soul, every other kind of leadership becomes overflow.

So lead yourself forward. One decision. One confession. One surrendered breath at a time. You are not behind - you're becoming. And every step toward obedience is a declaration that the old you no longer gives the orders.

Casting Off Weights

Hebrews 12:1 urges us: *"Throw off everything that hinders and the sin that so easily entangles, and run with perseverance the race marked out for us."*

Some of you are not losing because of sin - you are losing because of weights. They are not wicked, but they are heavy. They are the invisible loads you carry when no one is looking - the expectations of others, the echo of past mistakes, the fear of disappointing everyone who cheered for you.

Not every burden comes from rebellion; some come from responsibility that has morphed into identity. You were never meant to define yourself by what you carry.

Henri Nouwen called it "the burden of the self-rejecting heart." (Nouwen, 1992) [90] That phrase pierced me the first time I read it. Because that's what happens when you confuse calling with proving. You start trying to earn the love that was already given. You start serving to be seen instead of serving because you're loved. And before long, even good things - ministry, family, reputation - begin to feel like bricks in a backpack.

But Christ calls you *beloved*. The yoke you carry is not His, because His yoke is easy and His burden light (Matthew 11:30). When the race feels impossible, it may not be your strength that is failing - it may be the weights you refuse to release.

Weights disguise themselves as "should." I should be further by now. I should be stronger. I should have healed already. I should have pleased them. But *should* is a shackle when it replaces *surrender.*

God never called you to run with comparison strapped to your back. He called you to run light, run free, run loved. He doesn't measure speed; He measures surrender. He doesn't crown perfection; He crowns perseverance.

---

[90] Henri J.M. Nouwen, *Life of the Beloved* (New York: Crossroad, 1992)

You don't have to drag every expectation with you into this season. Lay them down. The race was never meant to be run carrying what He already carried for you.

If you could see how light you'd become once you let go, you'd drop the weight mid-sentence. Grace is not permission to keep running tired - it's power to run unchained.

So take a breath. Let go of what no longer belongs on your shoulders. You are not a beast of burden - you are a son, a daughter, a runner marked by grace. And Heaven is still cheering, "Lay it down, and run."

Full Circle: The Promise Kept

Do you remember the promise I whispered at the beginning of this book?

That you would learn to drop what has already been destroyed.

That you would refuse the prison of shame.

That you would walk unchained in your true design.

This is that moment.

Chains will still rattle. People will still try to fasten them back. You may even reach for them yourself. Their sound may echo in your memory, in the accusations of others, even in your own thoughts. But rattling is not binding. Noise is not power. Their power is gone. The prison door is open.

This is the sound of broken chains.

It is the sound of your freedom.

If you are not winning, it is not over. Because the truth has not changed: **you are Spirit-born. You are unchained.**

Pressing On

Freedom is not a finish line - it's a way of walking. You have come far, but the journey of the overcomer is not measured in miles; it is measured in *movement toward the Master.*

Paul said, *"I press on to take hold of that for which Christ Jesus took hold of me."* (Philippians 3:12) Even after miracles, after ministry, after chains fell and churches rose, Paul still pressed on. Because the victory we carry is not maintenance - it is momentum.

The enemy will still whisper. People may still reach for your wrists with old chains. But the Cross has already spoken the final verdict: *"It is finished."* (John 19:30) The only way a broken chain can bind again is if you choose to hold it.

You are the head, not the tail (Deuteronomy 28:13). You are more than a conqueror through Him who loves you (Romans 8:37). You are seated with Christ in heavenly places (Ephesians 2:6). And yet, freedom still calls for faithfulness. For even the righteous fall seven times, but rise again (Proverbs 24:16).

When others try to fasten old chains upon you, remember Joseph. His brothers sold him, his captors framed him, yet God used every chain as a chariot to destiny (Genesis 50:20). What they meant for evil, Heaven bent toward purpose.

When you are tempted to pick up your own chains - shame, fear, comparison - remember Peter. He wept over denial but found grace waiting on the shore (John 21:15-17). Love restored what failure tried to erase.

So drop the links that no longer belong to you. Shake off the dust of yesterday. Stand tall under the weight of grace.

Paul told the Corinthians, *"Thanks be to God, who gives us the victory through our Lord Jesus Christ."* (1 Corinthians 15:57) Notice: gives - not gave. Victory is not a memory; it is a movement. Every sunrise is another reminder that the grave is still empty.

You were born to live unburdened. To walk in joy unchained. To keep pressing until freedom becomes the rhythm of your breathing.

So lift your head, overcomer. The journey is not over. The final shout is coming. But today - right here - you can stand, free and fearless, in the echo of what has already been won.

You are Spirit-born. You are unchained. You are still pressing on.

Scripture Index

#Unchained

#SpiritBorn

#NeverAgain

Apostolic Equipping:

Multiplying Freedom

Freedom is never meant to end with you. Apostolic culture multiplies what it carries. When you help another stand, your own footing strengthens.

Every believer holds keys made from broken chains. Use them. Share your story - even the scars. Testimony becomes invitation. Walk with others until their hands grow steady and their hearts remember how to stand.

Freedom deepens when it's given away. The road you've walked becomes a map for someone still lost in the fog.

Kingdom Practices:
- Tell your freedom story to someone still fighting theirs.
- Pray with, not just for, those walking through struggle.
- Hand off small responsibilities - let others grow through trust.
- Treat every breakthrough as seed meant to be sown.

(Galatians 5:13) - *"Through love, serve one another."*

Chapter Seventeen

The Pearl and the Field God's System

I found myself at a time in my life when the career I had studied for and worked in for nearly two decades was suddenly cut. The job I had poured myself into was gone. The ministry doors I once walked through had dried up. Out of necessity, I started a construction company as a general contractor - right as the COVID pandemic began.

A year into the pandemic, I was adrift. The world itself seemed to be unraveling, and my family's life felt no less chaotic. I was alone. I was questioning. I was wondering where God was in the middle of the storm.

The First Whisper

It was during that season that God spoke to me in a way that unraveled my defenses. I was in the shower, heavy under the weight of loss and disappointment, when I heard Him say:

"You are My favorite."

That word was too much for me… and yet not enough to contain His heart.

I began to weep. Water poured over my face, but it wasn't only water. It was grief, and shame, and relief all mingled together.

My lips whispered back thanks. My heart swelled under the scandal of such love.

But then His voice returned:

"You are not My only favorite - they all are."

That word undid me. Not only was I seen, chosen, delighted in - but every son, every daughter, every broken soul was His favorite too. His heart is wide enough to hold us all as treasures, without diminishing the love He has for each one.

That encounter planted a seed in me. But He wasn't finished yet.

The Pearl and the Treasure

One night not long after, the Lord woke me from my sleep.

He said, *"You are a pearl of great price."*

I answered groggily, "Yes."

He said, *"You are a treasure in a field."*

I said, "Yes. The Kingdom is..."

Then His voice sharpened: *"Wake up and look it up."*

I got out of bed and opened the Scriptures to Matthew 13:44-46:

"The kingdom of heaven is like treasure hidden in a field. When a man found it, he hid it again, and in his joy went and sold all he had and bought that field. Again, the kingdom of heaven is like a merchant looking for

fine pearls. When he found one of great value, he went away and sold everything he had and bought it."

I read it and whispered to Him: "The kingdom is like a pearl of great price."

He said, *"No. Read it again."*

I read it again. "The kingdom is like a treasure in the field."

He said, *"No. Read it again."*

I read it again.

Finally, when I still did not understand, He spoke with clarity that pierced me to my bones:

"I am the man. And you are the treasure. I left everything to come and find you."

I sat in awe. The words sank deeper than my bones. I had always imagined myself as the seeker, striving to buy the pearl. But in that moment, I realized I was not the merchant - I was the pearl. I was not the buyer - I was the treasure.

That night, my chains of striving clattered to the ground. The shame of striving, the weight of proving, the fear of not being enough - all of it shattered in the light of His words.

The Revelation

For years, I had believed the parable was about *my* pursuit of Him - my willingness to sell all to gain Christ. But that night, He turned it upside down and showed me what I could not see: *He* is the one who gave everything. *He* is the one who left Heaven.

He is the one who bought the whole field to claim the treasure hidden there.

And the treasure… was me.

Not the polished me. Not the ministry me. Not the version of me that knows the right verses and hides the wrong scars. The treasure was the me buried in mud, tangled in weeds, unseen beneath the soil. The me that I would be when shaped by the Master to grow into the Full Stature of His Son.

I am the pearl. I am the treasure. But pearls don't form without pressure, and treasures don't shine without uncovering.

When He found me, I was still covered in the dirt of what I'd walked through. But He didn't flinch. He didn't bargain. He bought the *whole field* - the mess, the history, the hidden corners - because redemption doesn't negotiate partial ownership.

He saw not just who I was, but who I could become in His hands. The treasure wasn't my perfection; it was my potential. The pearl had value from the start, but it needed a jeweler's touch to reveal its radiance. And in His hands - the hands that shaped galaxies and washed feet - my rough edges became reflection.

He left everything to find me. And now He is still refining me, polishing the places that pain once dulled, cutting away what hides the shine. I am the treasure not because I glimmered in the field, but because His grace refused to leave me buried there.

He didn't just redeem me - He restored my function. He didn't just uncover my worth - He revealed my purpose.

I am the treasure, yes... but only because I belong to the One who knew its worth before anyone else could see it

A Treasure Till the End

And if you think it's too late for you - let me tell you another story.

One afternoon the Lord spoke to me and told me to go to my great-aunt's house. He said, "Tell her she is about to go home, but she has one last task to do."

Alzheimer's had been stealing pieces of her - names slipped and songs faded - but when I knocked and the family let me in she looked straight at me and said, *"The preacher is here for me."*

What amazed me was this: even though her memory struggled, something in her spirit told her it was time. She knew when I arrived that heaven's clock was striking. She was not afraid; she was expectant.

I told her what the Lord had said. I told her she needed to call her descendants together and pray a blessing over each of them before she could go - just as Jacob had called his sons and laid hands upon them (Genesis 48-49).

Here is what amazed me even more: she did not pass that week, or even that month. The Lord gave her six more months of life. Six months of grace. Six months so her children, grandchildren, and even far-off relatives could travel home. And when they gathered, the disease that had clouded her mind seemed to part like mist. She knew them. She laid her hands on them. She spoke blessing, name by name, face by face.

The family told me later that this time was a miracle. God unchained her mind long enough to finish the task He had set before her. What looked like an ending was turned into an extension. Where we saw decline, God saw destiny.

For those who whisper, 'It's too late for me,' her story is your proof that chains of time itself can be broken. Her story is for anyone who believes it's too late: God can stretch time, break chains, and reveal your worth even at the edge of life. He will not abandon His treasure.

For You Too

This is not just my story. It is yours too.

You are the pearl. You are the treasure hidden in the field. Christ sold all - His very life - to buy you back. You are the joy set before Him (Hebrews 12:2). You are precious and honored in His sight (Isaiah 43:4).

Others may still try to chain you to your past. You may even keep reaching for broken links of shame and guilt. But His declaration is stronger: *"I left everything for you."*

Full-Circle Echo

At the very beginning of this book, I told you that people will try to put chains back on you. I told you that some chains are carried long after they've been broken, rattling like ghosts at your feet, trying to convince you they still have power.

This final word is the answer to that first cry. The chains fall - the ting of cold iron striking the ground - because the treasure has already been claimed.

You are not defined by what once bound you. You are not sentenced to drag around links that Christ has already shattered.

The kingdom is not a prison. It is a field. And buried in that field - in the dirt, in the mud, in the forgotten places - was treasure. Christ saw it. Christ saw you. And He gave all He had to buy the field, not for the soil, but for the treasure hidden inside.

The story that began with broken chains ends here with unveiled treasure.

The same voice that once whispered, *"Drop what has already been destroyed,"* now declares, *"You are the pearl. You are the treasure. I left everything to find you."*

Chains mark the beginning. Treasure marks the end. And in between, your life - your scars, your tears, your surrender - becomes living proof of His unrelenting love.

Now the story comes full circle. The first sound was the clatter of chains falling - links rattling like thunder as shame lost its grip. That sound echoes through eternity. And the last sound is treasure revealed - the echo not of bondage, but of belonging.

This is how you remember: not by the rattles at your feet, but by the price He paid to claim you as His pearl.

The Treasure and the Pearl

Heaven's story has always been about pursuit. Not of perfection, but of you.

From Eden's garden to Calvary's hill, the voice of God has echoed one truth: You are the treasure in the field. You are the pearl worth everything.

For years you may have believed the parable was about your pursuit of Him - your willingness to sell all to gain Christ. But look again. The revelation has always been reversed.

He is the man who sold all. He is the merchant who left the marketplace of heaven. He is the One who saw your worth when you were buried in the dirt, hidden beneath shame, covered by years of failure and fear. And He bought the whole field just to get to you. (Matthew 13:44-46)

The treasure was not perfect. It was not polished. It was covered in mud, tangled in roots, wrapped in history. But He saw beyond the soil - to the glory still buried within.

That's the gospel. He didn't die to make you valuable; He died because you already were. He didn't purchase you as property; He redeemed you as family. You were the joy set before Him (Hebrews 12:2).

You are the treasure that cost heaven everything. The pearl purchased through pierced hands. The inheritance He refused to live without.

215

Paul wrote, *"While we were still sinners, Christ died for us."* (Romans 5:8) He did not wait for your worth to appear - He called it forth by His own blood. He bought the whole field - thorns, stones, and all - just to resurrect the hidden beauty within.

And now, as the dirt falls away, the shine of what He saw all along begins to emerge. You are not defined by the soil that once hid you, but by the Spirit that now fills you. You are not an echo of your past; you are the evidence of His promise. You are Spirit-born. You are unchained. You are His.

So stand tall, pearl of great price. Let the sound at your feet remind you - not of bondage, but of broken chains singing freedom's song. The gates of your past are open, and the road ahead is radiant with purpose. Your story is not finished; it is just beginning. The grave is behind you, and glory is before you.

The Gardener has reclaimed His field. The Merchant has found His pearl. The Father has come home to His treasure - and that treasure is you.

Final Invocation

In the name of Jesus Christ - the Chain-Breaker, the Field-Buyer, the Pearl-Collector, the Redeemer of all things lost - I declare over you:

Your chains are broken. Your shame is silenced. Your name is restored.

You will not wear the garments of grief. You will not speak the language of loss. You will not return to the prisons you have outgrown.

Every false identity falls now in the presence of truth. Every counterfeit crown is replaced by sonship. Every chain that ever dared to claim you is shattered beneath the weight of His glory.

You are the righteousness of God in Christ Jesus (2 Corinthians 5:21). You are seated with Him in heavenly places (Ephesians 2:6). You are a new creation; the old has passed away, the new has come (2 Corinthians 5:17). You are not a servant begging at the door - you are a son, a daughter, seated at the table (Romans 8:15-17).

From this moment forward: Walk as one who is loved. Speak as one who is free. Live as one who is home.

For the Spirit of the Lord is upon you - to proclaim liberty to the captives, to open prison doors, to restore sight to the blind, to announce the acceptable year of the Lord (Luke 4:18-19).

The grave is behind you. The Kingdom is within you. The world ahead of you waits to be transformed by the culture of Heaven you carry.

You are Spirit-born. You are unchained. You are the Father's treasure, the Son's joy, and the Spirit's dwelling place.

So go - terraform culture, awaken sons, and let freedom ring through your steps. Because the story of *Unchained* does not end here. It begins with you.

I declare this by the authority of the Word of God in the name of the Lord Jesus Christ.

Amen and amen.

#SpiritBorn #Unchained #ThePearl #FreedomLives

Scripture Index

#SpiritBorn

#Unchained

#ThePearl

Apostolic Equipping:

Remembering Together

Apostolic community grows by remembering - not the weight of chains, but the sound they made when they fell. The Kingdom is sustained by gratitude, not amnesia.

Every believer carries a "pearl story" - the moment heaven called their name and dirt gave way to glory. When we share those stories, freedom multiplies. Testimony becomes atmosphere. Gratitude becomes gravity.

We don't tell our stories to exalt ourselves, but to magnify the One who sold everything to claim us. Remembering is not nostalgia; it is prophecy. It declares, *"The same God who freed me will free you."*

Kingdom Practices:
- Share your chain-breaking moment with someone.
- Listen to theirs like it's holy ground.
- Mark anniversaries of freedom together until remembrance becomes your rhythm.

(Psalm 77:11-12) - *"I will remember the deeds of the Lord."*

Bibliography

Austin-Sparks, T. (1950). *The Centrality and Supremacy of the Lord Jesus Christ*. Witness and Testimony Publishers.

Barber, E. W. (1991). *Prehistoric Textiles: The Development of Cloth in the Neolithic and Bronze Ages with Special Reference to the Aegean*. Princeton University Press.

Brunschwig, J. (1986). *Ancient Roman Punishments*. CNRS.

Chambers, O. (1935). *My Utmost for His Highest*. Dodd, Mead & Co.

Dillard, A. (1989). *The Writing Life*. Harper & Row.

Elder, P. the. (1945). *Natural History*. Harvard University Press.

Frazer, J. G. (1890). *The Golden Bough*. Macmillan.

Keller, T. (2011). *The Meaning of Marriage*. Dutton.

Lewis, C. S. (1942). *The Screwtape Letters*. HarperOne.

Lewis, C. S. (1952). *Mere Christianity*. Geoffrey Bles.

Lewis, C. S. (1970). *God in the Dock: Essays on Theology and Ethics*. Eerdmans.

Lewis, C. S. (2006). *Collected Letters, Vol. 3*. HarperSanFrancisco.

Manning, B. (1994). *Abba's Child: The Cry of the Heart for Intimate Belonging*. NavPress.

Manning, B. (2005). *The Ragamuffin Gospel: Good news for the bedraggled, beat-up, and burnt-out*. Multnomah Publishing.

Murray, A. (1982). *Absolute Surrender*. Whitaker House.

Nee, W. (1961). *The Normal Christian Life*. Tyndale House.

Nouwen, H. J. M. (1974). *Out of Solitude: Three Meditations on the Christian Life*. Ave Maria Press.

Nouwen, H. J. M. (1981a). *Making All Things New: An Invitation to the Spiritual Life*. HarperOne.

Nouwen, H. J. M. (1981b). *The Way of the Heart*. HarperOne.

Nouwen, H. J. M. (1992). *Life of the Beloved*. Crossroad Publishing.

Packer, J. I. (1973). *Knowing God*. InterVarsity Press.

Rice, K. M. (2023a). *Cultivating the New Nature: Growing into the Full Stature of Christ*. Eternal Kingdom International Publishing, LLC.

Rice, K. M. (2023b). *The Noah Generation: The Sign of Revival Rain*. Eternal Kingdom International Publishing, LLC.

Ten Boom, C. (1982). *Clippings from My Notebook*. Fleming H. Revell.

Tozer, A. W. (1948). *The Pursuit of God*. Christian Publications.

Tozer, A. W. (1955). *The Root of the Righteous*. Moody Publishers.

Tozer, A. W. (1960). *Of God and Men*. Christian Publications.

Tozer, A. W. (1961). *The Knowledge of the Holy*. HarperCollins.

Virgil. (1990). *The Aeneid*. Vintage Classics.

Webb, D. (2025a). *Building the Kingdom Through the Local Church*. Eternal Kingdom International Publishing, LLC.

Webb, D. (2025b). *Escape the Shame of Babylon*. Eternal Kingdom International Publishing, LLC.

Webb, D. (2025c). *The Unique Factor*. Eternal Kingdom International Publishing, LLC.

Willard, D. (2002). *Renovation of the Heart: Putting on the Character of Christ*. MavPress.

Glossary of Terms

Adoption

To be brought into the family of God through the Spirit, no longer as slaves but as sons and daughters.
Scripture: Romans 8:15-17; Galatians 4:5-7; Ephesians 1:5

Anointing

The empowerment and presence of the Holy Spirit that marks and equips believers for purpose and service.
Scripture: 1 John 2:27; Isaiah 61:1; Acts 10:38

Apostolic Culture

A Kingdom environment built by servant-leaders who multiply freedom, community, and transformation.
Scripture: Acts 2:42-47; Ephesians 4:11-13; 2 Timothy 2:2

Babylon

A metaphor for worldly systems - political, cultural, or religious - that enslave people through pride, greed, and performance.
Scripture: Revelation 18:1-4; Jeremiah 51:6-7; 1 John 2:15-17

Beloved

The identity of every believer as deeply loved by God, chosen not for performance but relationship.

Scripture: Song of Solomon 6:3; Matthew 3:17;
Ephesians 5:1-2

Chains

Symbol of bondage - sin, shame, fear, or systems that keep
believers from walking in Spirit-born freedom.
Scripture: Acts 12:7; Isaiah 61:1; Galatians 5:1

Culture of Heaven

The atmosphere and value system of the Kingdom of God
- love, righteousness, peace, and joy in the Spirit -
manifested on earth through believers.
Scripture: Romans 14:17; Matthew 6:10; Philippians
3:20

Declaration

A spoken confession that aligns the believer's identity with
God's truth rather than the lies of the old nature.
Scripture: Proverbs 18:21; Romans 10:9-10; 2
Corinthians 4:13

Emulation

The sinful imitation of another person's anointing or
calling, rather than living authentically in one's own.
Scripture: Galatians 5:20 (ζῆλος - *zēlos*); John 21:21-22

Faith

Active trust in God's character that acts beyond emotion
or circumstance.
Scripture: Hebrews 11:1; 2 Corinthians 5:7; James 2:17

Feelings

Emotional responses that reveal the state of the soul; they are valid but must be led by the Spirit.

Scripture: Psalm 42:5; Hebrews 4:15; Matthew 26:38-39

Freedom

The state of walking in the Spirit's power, free from sin's dominion and from self-imposed bondage.

Scripture: John 8:36; Galatians 5:1; Romans 8:2

Garden / Terraforming

Metaphor for restoring earth to its original Kingdom design - cultivating environments where heaven and earth intersect.

Scripture: Genesis 2:15; Romans 8:19-21; Isaiah 58:12

Identity

The believer's new nature in Christ - Spirit-born, beloved, and commissioned to reflect His image.

Scripture: 2 Corinthians 5:17; Colossians 3:10; 1 Peter 2:9

Kingdom

God's active reign and rule expressed through His people on earth as it is in heaven.

Scripture: Matthew 6:33; Luke 17:21; Romans 14:17

New Nature

The regenerated self birthed through repentance, baptism,
and indwelt by the Holy Spirit, replacing the old nature
of sin.

Scripture: Ephesians 4:22-24; Colossians 3:9 - 10;
Romans 6:4

Old Man (Old Nature)

The fallen self ruled by sin and self-effort, crucified with
Christ at salvation.

Scripture: Romans 6:6; Galatians 2:20; Colossians 3:9

Presence

The manifest nearness of God that brings transformation,
rest, and direction.

Scripture: Exodus 33:14-15; Psalm 16:11; Acts 3:19

Redemption

The act of being purchased and restored by Christ's blood;
the foundation of all freedom.

Scripture: 1 Peter 1:18-19; Ephesians 1:7; Colossians
1:13-14

Resurrection Life

The power that raised Jesus from the dead now active in
the believer, bringing new life to every area once dead.

Scripture: Romans 8:11; Philippians 3:10; John 11:25-26

Shame

The false verdict that defines identity by past failure rather than by grace; the opposite of sonship.

Scripture: Genesis 3:10; Isaiah 54:4; Romans 8:1

Spirit-Born

A believer reborn through the Holy Spirit into divine nature and Kingdom identity.

Scripture: John 3:5-8; Romans 8:9-11; Titus 3:5

Struggle

The tension between flesh and Spirit that reveals growth, not failure; the proving ground of freedom.

Scripture: Galatians 5:17; Romans 7:19-25; James 1:2-4

Transformation

The ongoing process of becoming like Christ through the renewing of the mind and the indwelling of the Spirit.

Scripture: Romans 12:2; 2 Corinthians 3:18; Philippians 1:6

Treasure / The Pearl

Metaphor for the believer as the object of Christ's redeeming love - the one for whom He sold all to purchase.

Scripture: Matthew 13:44-46; Isaiah 43:4; 1 John 4:9 - 10

Unchained

A prophetic declaration of freedom - no longer bound by
sin, shame, fear, or worldly systems; living as a restored
image-bearer of God.

Scripture: John 8:36; Galatians 5:1; Colossians 2:14-15

.

Thematic Word Index

Scripture Index

Old Testament

Genesis

Exodus

Numbers

Deuteronomy

Joshua

Judges

1 Samuel

1 Kings

2 Kings

2 Chronicles

Psalms

New Testament

239

240

Other Good Books

from EKI Publishing

www.ekibooks.com

- *The Unique Factor*
  - o   By David Webb
- *Escape the Shame of Babylon*
  - o   By David Webb
- *Building the Kingdom Through the Local Church*
  - o   By David Webb
- *Unchained: Freed to be His Treasure*
  - o   By Kirkland M. Rite
- *Baptized: Why did I get Wet*
  - o   By Kirland M. Rite

Coming from Eternal Kingdom
International Publishing

January 2026

Baptized
By Kirkland M. Rite

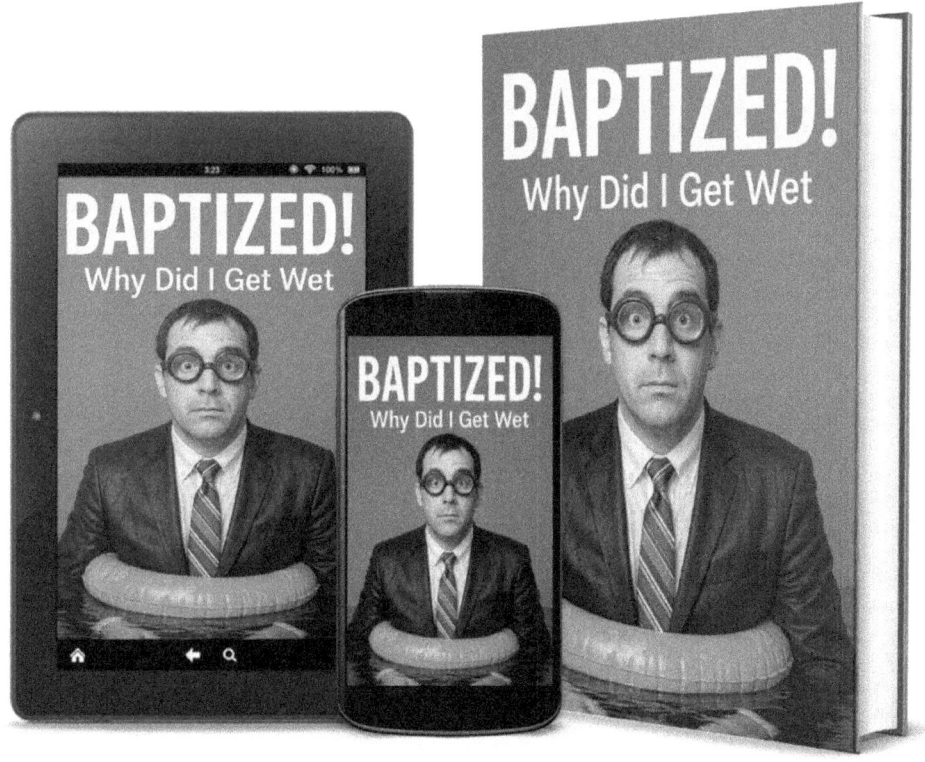

www.ingramcontent.com/pod-product-compliance
Lightning Source LLC
Chambersburg PA
CBHW061611120626
46550CB00004B/1683